EXCELLENCE TETF

EXPLAINED

By

Professor Mohamed Zairi

European Centre for
Best Practice Management

PUBLISHING HOUSE

Excellence Tetralogy
Explained

1st Edition 2010

ISBN 978-1-906993-08-5

9 781906 993085 >

Published by:
European Centre for Best Practice Management
Holly House | Spring Gardens Lane | Keighley | BD20 6LE | UK
Tele: +44 (0) 1535 612060 | Web: www.ECBPM.com
Email: books@ecbpm.com

Printers
Inprint + Design Ltd
WB07 Richmond Building | Carlton Street | Bradford | BD7 1DP |UK
Tele: +44 (0) 1274 235757 | Web: http://www.inprintdesign.com/

Table of Contents

Table of Figures

Acknowledgements

No book is ever written alone and no research endeavour is ever carried out in solitude.

First and foremost, my greatest appreciation has to go to my research teams past and present, and in particular, the individuals involved in these compilations and whose research projects I have enjoyed leading and closely supervising.

My sincere thanks also go to my support teams, past and present, who make our work possible every day of the week, all months of the year and who have helped sustain our focus and our determination to continue pioneering.

Lastly, my thanks and appreciation goes to my wife Alweena and my children Adel, Bilal and Nadir for their unconditional love and unwavering support.

Dedication

But when I searched, I found no work so meritorious as the discovery and development of the arts and inventions that tend to civilise the life of man.

Francis Bacon

This book is dedicated to all the men and women whose mission in life is to pioneer, validate and enlighten others with knowledge and the discovery of facts and the truth. It is also dedicated to all those who can help by developing solutions to problems and finding answers to enquiries. Dr Joseph Juran once said: 'My job of contributing to the welfare of my fellow man is the great unfinished business.' It is therefore hoped that the content of this book will help move forward the human thinking capacity, will assist in the development of the enquiry mind and will support future quests for knowledge and advancement of theory and practice in the field of Total Quality Management and related topics.

Our biggest thrill would be to see that the content of this book is used, the knowledge presented consumed and the various ideas applied. It may of course be wishful thinking but we remain hopeful that the efforts made in putting this text together are not futile and that there will be some positive use of the various concepts presented.

As Rita C. Richey (October, 1999) wrote *"Ideas often take a substantial amount of time to be appreciated, and even for those few that attract attention quickly, there is an assumption that one needs the perspective of hindsight to determine their lasting value. Consequently, an intellectual inheritance is usually determined by the survivors rather than by the donor, and the labels that describe the merit of one's ideas are affixed by subsequent generations."*

Excellence Tetralogy Explained

Tetralogy is thought to come from the ancient Greek dramatic festivals where different plays were presented in the form of tetralogies. It is also reported during the time of Shakespeare where his major plays were presented in the form of tetralogies. Shakespeare's major history plays fell into two different tetralogies. The first comprising the three parts of Henry VI and Richard III, the second comprising Richard II, Henry IV, parts 1 and 2, and Henry V. Lawrence Durrell's (1957-60) 'Alexandra' quartet is also a tetralogy of novels. The real inspiration for coining the term 'Excellence Tetralogy' has come from the work of Dr Joseph Juran, who coined the term 'Juran Trilogy' in some of his major works on quality. The Juran Trilogy will be explained in the following sections. However, it has been an extremely useful philosophy in promoting the application of total quality management as an integrated concept, and Juran has supported his Trilogy with tools and techniques that have enabled organisations to apply the principles of quality, to optimise their capability for delivering quality and value to their customers. Excellence Tetralogy, therefore, is an integrated concept that is made up of four sub-elements that are all interdependent, operating in harmony and creating a holistic model approach to delivering business success.

Excellence Tetralogy is the result of significant research work that has been undertaken for a sustained period exceeding 20 years. Most of the elements proposed in the Excellence Tetralogy approach have been empirically tested and validated in most sectors of the economy and using different geographical contexts in various parts of the world. The Excellence Tetralogy, as opposed to Juran's Trilogy, is more concerned with the wider perspective of building the external business capability for sustaining itself and delivering expected growth and development. The Juran Trilogy is more concerned with internal optimisation for enabling businesses to build internal capabilities, so as to deliver consistently, reliably and confidently to the customer. The Excellence Tetralogy does not nullify the importance of Juran's Trilogy, but perhaps it is an opportunity to build upon the work of total quality management in enabling businesses internally to a higher level of operation, where the ethos is more on holistically creating organisations that are fit to operate for the short term and capable of ensuring their future survivability and continuity.

The Juran Trilogy revisited

The Juran Trilogy was developed back in the early 1950s and was based on research undertaken by Dr Joseph Juran. It has been used all over the world and has guided organisations to learn how to improve internal quality in order to maximise customer satisfaction, and also how to deal with the minimisation of dissatisfaction by reducing deficiencies and eliminating costs due to poor quality and waste. In a sense the legacy of the Juran Trilogy was to help change the culture of businesses. It has helped empower employees to be pro-active in understanding what customer needs are and how to satisfy them. It was also helpful in guiding organisations with the focus on providing quality services and quality products to their customers through improving deficiency base (lean) and the effectiveness base, which is a true measure of quality. Through a dynamic approach of information flow as a result of the problem solving opportunity that the Trilogy offers, employees can minimise problems, pin down causes and optimise quality. The Trilogy itself is made up of three major components: quality planning, quality control and quality improvement.

Quality planning

This process is to help determine customer needs and develop processes and methods that are required to meet or exceed customer needs. In later years these processes have been referred to as Design for Six Sigma, or Concurrent Engineering. The challenge for quality planning in any organisation is to identify the most important needs of their customers. These are the steps that Dr Juran put in place:

- Identify who the customers are.

- Determine the needs of those customers.

- Translate those needs into technical language.

- Develop a product or service that corresponds to those needs.

- Optimise the product or service features, so as to meet the technical needs and the customer requirements.

Quality control

The purpose of quality control is to ensure that the process is running in an optimum and effective manner. This will ensure that at any level where there is chronic waste in the process, the problem is contained and is not allowed to get worse. Chronic waste, as argued by Dr Juran, is the real cause for high costs of poor quality that can exist in any process. These chronic wastes may exist due to a wide variety of factors, including deficiency in planning, for example. If ignored quality waste could cost organisations a significant amount of money from re-work, time spent on dealing with complaints and recovering from customer dissatisfaction. If the waste is allowed to get worse, Dr Juran describes this as the sporadic spike. He suggests that teams are put together to deal with corrective action in order to identify the causes that have led to this abnormal variation and to treat the causes so the corrections can bring the process back into the zone that he describes as 'the quality control limit zone'. Dr Juran suggests the following:

- Prove that the process can produce the product or the service under operating conditions with minimal inspection.

- Transfer the process to operation.

Quality improvement

The elimination of defects and waste and rework that can impact positively on the improvement of processes is ultimately going to reduce the cost of poor quality. Once processes have been challenged and continuously improved, these will become capable, and will have predictable outcomes. Dr Juran argues that in these conditions the improvements are the reasons for achieving tighter variation control and enabling processes to become capable. He calls this 'purposeful quality improvement' or breakthrough. Dr Juran suggested the following steps in relation to quality improvement:

- Develop a process which is able to produce a product.

- Optimise the process.

Excellence Tetralogy: Explained

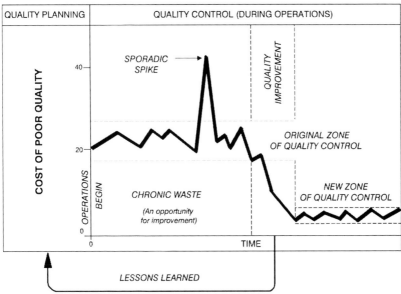

Figure 1: Juran Trilogy

Figure 1 illustrates the Juran Trilogy and the 3 elements that it is based upon. In addition, it also shows the dynamic nature of the Trilogy, which is the improvement that leads to lessons learned and new knowledge that can guide the quality planning activity and ensure that organisations improve quality upstream and tighten the specifications for customer requirements all the time through a Six Sigma oriented approach. Over the years the Juran Trilogy has helped thousands of businesses build internal sophistication and confidence, and tackle the rigorous requirements of their customers and the market in which they operate. The planning methodology, for instance, has enabled businesses all over the world to put in place strategic and tactical goals that can enable them to achieve their wide variety of goals and objectives with confidence. This has done so by total reliance on the internal capabilities that will enable them to focus on new innovations in terms of new products and services, and new levels of dealing with their customers with the full

5

confidence that quality is not going to be compromised. So quality planning has helped to establish high standards of performance and tighter specifications in terms of quality in product and processes. The control methodology on the other hand has been used to create a new mindset to prevent errors from happening, creating defects or blips in the system. This mindset of control has created internal confidence for recovery, for engaging the enquiring mind, for dealing with complaints from customers and for ensuring that an optimum performance, which is the desirable goal, is viable all of the time. Improvement methodology on the other hand, or what is referred to as the breakthrough methodology, is to ensure that the plan, do, study, act process for the learning and innovation is driven pro-actively as a dynamic cycle for raising continuously the levels of organisational capability and performance, but also as a means by which new innovations are introduced, and breakthrough thinking is activated so that big leaps in performance can be achieved and higher levels of customer satisfaction can follow thereon.

Whilst the Juran Trilogy has in itself been a breakthrough in terms of quality thinking for over 50 years, it has nonetheless focused on the internal perspective of organisations. It has also focused mainly on organisational capabilities in terms of the 'push' perspective of the value chain. The Excellence Tetralogy is suggested to be an alternative to dealing with an internet based work environment, where the customer is not just a passive recipient but is considered to be the key stakeholder and is put in the driving seat so that a 'pull' mentality is put into effect.

Excellence Tetralogy: key elements

The Tetralogy model

The Excellence Tetralogy concept, as depicted in Figure 2, has four key inter-connected & inter-dependent elements associated with it.

- The leadership
- The capability
- The customer
- The business.

Figure 2: The Excellence Tetralogy model

7

The starting point for building sustainable and impactful business is to have the aforementioned elements working in harmony in order to deliver optimum performance and leveraging internally and externally in a dynamic fashion for the end benefit of customers and stakeholders. Figure 2 represents the model with the following key explanations.

1. Excellence Tetralogy as an emerging concept, seeks to drive organisations for a sustainable impact that is only realisable through extending the understanding of the business value chain, the refocus on customer centric practices and the redefinition of who the stakeholders are.

2. The underlying assumption used for the Excellence Tetralogy is that the four key elements have to co-exist and are truly and totally inter-dependent. The leadership component is the key driver of sustainable impact, whilst the capability element is the engine that furnishes the value aspect; the customer is the main focus in all organisational endeavours. Lastly, the business is a model of continuity and sustainability.

3. Excellence Tetralogy delivers true capabilities that strengthen the growth and development of business organisations as they evolve and mature in their respective markets. The research undertaken in recent years at the European Centre for Total Quality Management has revealed that there are possibly 13 business orientations that world class organisations tend to adopt in order to harness their internal capabilities and deliver sustainable results.

4. Excellence Tetralogy operates as a concept through the permeation of best practice and the injection of learning and innovation. As Figure 2 indicates, the growth of organisations in terms of performance, capability and knowledge thinking happened through a repeated cycle of learning, experimentation, change and transformation and the adoption of a cultural innovativeness.

Excellence Tetralogy: the leadership element

The model definition of effective leadership, as suggested in this text, is based on two dimensions:

- The ability to ensure constancy of purpose.

- The ability to stimulate growth.

Leadership in the modern context cannot be distracted from steering the organisations that they are responsible along the path to success, from the point of view of making useful and successful repeated journeys of realising competitive business performance on the one hand, but also the overall health and sustainability of the business has to be maintained for the long term. Here lies the main challenge for leaders:

- Should leaders bow to the demands of business shareholders, who demand quick results, repeated positive performances and healthy financial growth?

- Should leaders craft strategies that build on the past, that seek to maintain the purposefulness of the organisation in the long run?

- Should leaders try to compromise the strategic agenda by ensuring that they have a balanced perspective of delivering short term, whilst investing long term?

These three propositions cannot be treated in isolation. Leaders will have to use balanced judgment, scientific approaches based on information and analysis of markets, competition, customer feedback etc., and also they have to use cumulative experience on what makes sense and what pleases and delights the customer. Furthermore, leaders will have to use intuition and rely on newness and innovative thinking for stretching the competitive gain and maintaining a leadership position if they wish to do so. However, leaders will have to comply with a list of requirements that are thought to create a momentum for sustainable business growth, for the maintainability of purposefulness and in terms of continuity.

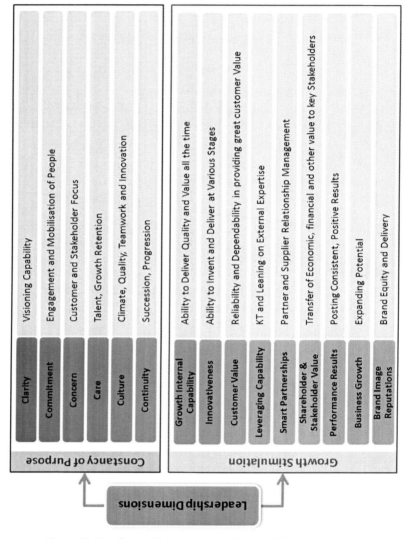

Figure 3: Excellence Tetralogy: the leadership element

Figure 3 illustrates the leadership element model in detail. In terms of constancy of purpose leaders are expected to undertake the following activities:

- *Clarity*: building visioning capability and ensuring its effective communication and organisational alignment.

- *Commitment*: the engagement and mobilisation of people is a challenge that must be undertaken in order to ensure total commitment to the vision, the mission and the strategic objectives.

- *Concern*: having an uncompromising focus on primary customers and other stakeholders

- *Care*: ensuring that people are grown and engaged, rewarded, recognised and retained, and also ensuring that there is a biased strategy towards talent.

- *Culture*: working on the instigation of a work climate that is enriched by quality of philosophy through the individual, teamwork contributions, and with an encouragement on problem solving approaches and the practice of innovative thinking.

- *Continuity*: ensuring that succession, on the one hand, protects the long term interests of the organisation through the inculcation of its values and guiding principles, but also ensuring progression in terms of growth and development within the organisation and outside.

In terms of the second challenge for leadership, it is their ability to stimulate growth at various levels and ensure that the businesses are set to do what is expected of them and they can deliver to the expectations of the various stakeholders. For this, leaders of the 21st century are expected to focus on the following key activities:

- **Growth of internal capability**: this means the ability to deliver quality and value all the time and to create dependability and reliability.

- **Innovativeness**: the ability to invent and deliver at various stages. This means creating a culture which is propelled forward by innovative thinking and a process oriented approach that welcomes new ideas and knows how to drive them and translate them into tangible outcomes that can excite the customer at the end.

- **Customer value**: making sure that the measurability of value is in terms of reliability and dependability, and making sure that the customer value is outside in and not measured internally only.

- **Leveraging capability**: encouraging knowledge transfer and learning and harnessing of external expertise.

- **Smart partnerships**: build supplier relationship management capabilities and a smart approach to fostering partnerships that can facilitate knowledge transfer and leveraging.

- **Shareholder and stakeholder value**: ensuring that the outcomes are fit for the purpose in terms of the transfer of financial and economic values as well as other means of satisfying stakeholder expectations.

- **Performance results**: being able to post consistent and positive results year in, year out.

- **Business growth**: being able to grow the potential of the business and exploit opportunities available in various parts of the world.

- **Brand image and reputation**: building brand equity and delivering the promise in a consistent and trustworthy manner.

Excellence Tetralogy: the capability element

There are numerous studies that have looked at business capabilities and their impact on business performance. A large number of studies have looked at the impact of individual capabilities and how these have been directly correlated and tested to prove their significance in terms of impact on internal performance and external business results. However, an emerging concept has been the study of interrelated capabilities and their impact on business performance. For instance, the work carried out by Martinette *et al.* (2003) argued about the importance of delivering received customer value and received shareholder value from the point of view of driving interrelated and inter-dependent blend of capabilities, including marketing orientation, business process orientation and perceived value amongst others. In recent times a study done at the European Centre for TQM (Battor, 2008) looked at the following capabilities: market orientation, learning orientation, innovation and customer relationship management (CRM), and it was established that these were considered to be key drivers of a sustainable business performance, and the results demonstrated that the linkages between the various capabilities impact directly on the enhancement of external business performance.

In the context of the Excellence Tetralogy concept, it has been argued that business performance, which is defined as a relative concept, and has to be looked at in the context of sustainable performance and continuity of the business itself, is heavily dependent on a wide variety of orientations that need to be introduced within the business in a systematic way, nurtured and developed in the minds of employees, converted into practices, built in the operating systems and exploited to the full, so as to provide value internally and externally. Once these orientations are translated into practices that are impactful they automatically become labelled as capabilities. The Excellence Tetralogy does therefore suggest that capabilities are not direct adoptions and there is a life cycle that needs to be observed before inherent capabilities are built and are made to impact in the right way. Whilst, for instance, focus on profit has been a major concern for most leaders, and no one argues that this is not indispensable, of course, nevertheless it can be argued that value creation, which is the desirable outcome that guarantees business success in the long term, is more of a priority than delivering short term profits. To understand further the importance of value creation it is therefore important to take organisations from a systems thinking perspective and look at the dynamics involved in the management of the entire organisation using resources, processes, methods, hard assets, technology, the flow of information and knowledge, the pool of know-how and talent available, and all of this guided from smart strategies and an approach to planning and deployment that can create alignment.

© Zairi, ECTQM, 2009

Figure 4: Excellence Tetralogy: the capability element

14

Figure 4 illustrates the capability element of the Excellence Tetralogy as a concept and it argues the following logic:

Orientations

This means that businesses operate in a dynamic fashion by observing knowledge and practices that can enhance their capabilities at various stages of the value chain. Furthermore, in a knowledge based work environment, it is argued that orientation is a relative concept, and that businesses will have to adapt to the external environment and readjust the leaning on what is right in terms of capabilities and strengths so as to remain effective and capable for competing externally. The notion of business orientation as a holistic, integrated concept is one that will become more pervasive in the 21st century. For a start, it is important that amongst all the various possible orientations that ultimately will lead to capabilities, the main focus should be on value. Value cannot therefore be considered just an abstract and economic concept; it should be seen as a driving force behind which decisions can be made at all levels within the organisation.

Woodruff (1997) defines customer value as follows:

The emotional bond established between a customer and producer, after the customer has used the salient product or service produced by that supplier, and found the product to be added value.

Woodruff (1997) continues to say that in relation to customer driven concept of value, the following definition is meaningful and useful:

Customer value is a customer's perceived preference for and evaluation of those product attributes, attribute performances, and consequences arising from use that facilitate (or block) achieving the customer's goals and purposes in use situations.

Outcomes

The outcomes of business orientations are several. At the heart of developing a new business mindset is to enhance core capabilities that can support organisations with their competitiveness and with their ability to satisfy the requirements of their key customers and other stakeholders. It is also possible that new management or business orientations can be adjusted to help reinforce the customer centric culture of the organisation. Furthermore, many organisations refresh their knowledge residue and bring in new concepts to ensure that there is total commitment towards the future and the new visions being implemented. Another reason for the adoption of new concepts is to enhance competitiveness. Furthermore, it is to create constancy and continuity by re-emphasising the core elements of the business and its guiding principles.

Capability elements

The Excellence Tetralogy capability element suggests that there are four possible directions used by businesses in order to secure their continuity and future prosperity.

- *The vision mindset*: this is to create alignment and ensure that there is total realignment behind the future direction of the business.

- *Management paradigm*: through the focus on key core capabilities new orientations are used to produce new paradigms or force existing paradigms through a re-engineering or a re-design perspective.

- *Value proposition*: to ensure that the culture, the climate and the human mindset is focused on the right value proposition. This approach is done through a re-emphasising approach.

- **Competitive standards**: by emphasising constancy, continuity and competitiveness, businesses will ensure that their focus will remain on creating and maintaining a competitive advantage. This practice is done through realising the benefits with intention and ensuring that all the strategic goals and objectives do materialise.

Business orientation gets rid of inertia and helps build positive momentum. The ability of organisations to reinvent themselves, rejuvenate, replenish their stock of knowledge and know how is vital for the survivability

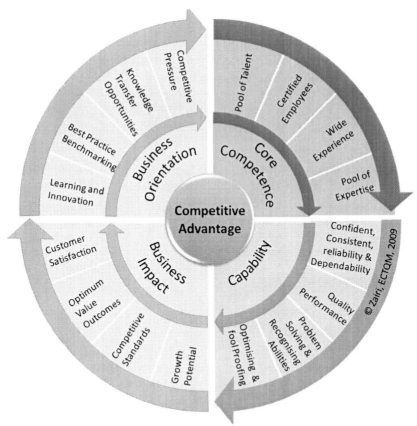

Figure 5: Capability conversion process

Figure 5 illustrates the capability conversion process as a closed loop cycle. The focus is on creating a sustainable competitive advantage and this is done by adopting a philosophy of business orientation for reasons which are proactive or reactive, dealing for instance with external competitive pressures or through wanting to expand the capacity of learning and innovation and the transfer of best practice through benchmarking, for instance. As argued previously, the business orientations have to be instigated, learned, applied, experimented with and applied across the board, and this could be to enhance pools of talent, ensuring that in the core areas of the organisation there is a sufficient number of employees certified, or even to widen the experience. Once core competencies are applied effectively and they start to become impactful at a competitive level, then they will become capabilities. Capabilities have to be demonstrated by being able to confidently, consistently and reliably deliver to the customer, having superior quality performance standards, being able to recover from service failures, having problem solving abilities and being able to optimise and foolproof at Six Sigma level. Core capabilities can impact in a relative manner on business performance for creating growth potential, all the way to creating customer satisfaction and loyalty.

Excellence Tetralogy: the customer element

The third element of the Excellence Tetralogy is perhaps the most important element, and concerns the evolution of customer mentality and the emergence of the tribal customer. The implications of internet technology has meant that the adoption of the customer centric commerce philosophy has shifted from a drive towards fulfilling the tangible transactional needs of customers and delivering the economics of companies towards focusing on improving the economies of the individuals instead (Figure 6).

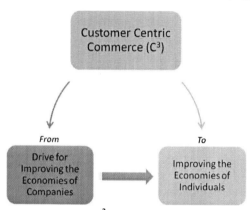

Figure 6: C^3 – A paradigm shift

This means that truly the customer has to be considered king. The customer needs and wants to interact through various touch points on a wide range of perspectives, including the following:

- Current products and services – in relation to existing provision levels the customer may wish to give feedback and evaluate the impactfulness of what they receive from their provider.

- Customers are becoming savvy and are starting to influence the future value proposition and want to influence future visions for product or service design, methods of delivery, and teach us functionalities and even appeal.

- The experience – here the customer takes the driving seat and wants to make his or her own decisions on the life cycle perspective of innovation development all the way to delivery and fulfilment.

- The brand – the transition here is that the customer uses the brand for various requirements. These could include emotional fulfilment, spiritual fulfilment, or even for other perspectives, such as social interactions to customer relationships (Figure 7).

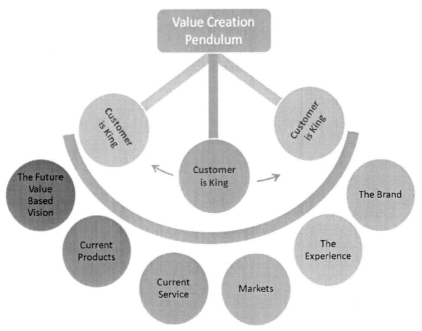

Figure 7: 'Customer is king' philosophy

The customer oriental transformational thinking in the context of the Excellence Tetralogy, argues that a shift is gradually taking place from a profit motive characterised by a 'push' firm-dominant practice into more a value based motive which is focused on the customer, and as argued previously, into a social motive where customer to customer practice is the norm. As Figure 8 depicts the move from a market 'push' philosophy to a customer 'pull' philosophy and ultimately to a customer driven relationship, is the challenge for the future.

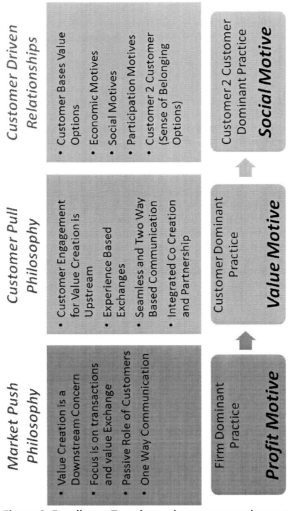

Figure 8: Excellence Tetralogy: the customer element

21

The challenge for organisations seeking to become truly excellent, therefore, is to radically change from a value creation approach which is more based on transactions and value chains, where the customer is treated as the passive recipient, and where communication is a one way channel only, into experience based exchanges, where customers are valued and actively engaged and empowered. This approach (customer pull) is driven by seamless and two way based communication. Ultimately, having an integrated co-creation and partnership mindset where customers can be even more engaged beyond the economics of business into social motives that concern them and concern them only. The challenge for businesses in the future, therefore, is to create a new type of differentiation away from products and services that hitherto have been concerned with hedonic fulfilment. This will become a baseline dimension only. By dealing with products and services and positioning them as good as the competition, or better than the competition, or even at 'best in class' level, this will no longer be sufficient for creating sustainable competition (Figure 9).

The proposed differentiation through the Excellence Tetralogy is based on real customer value and that is driven by the achievement of emotional fulfilment. This means that the experience route will start to tackle and fulfil needs and move away from just customising options into providing unique and extremely fulfilling experiences and generating true expressions of loyalty.

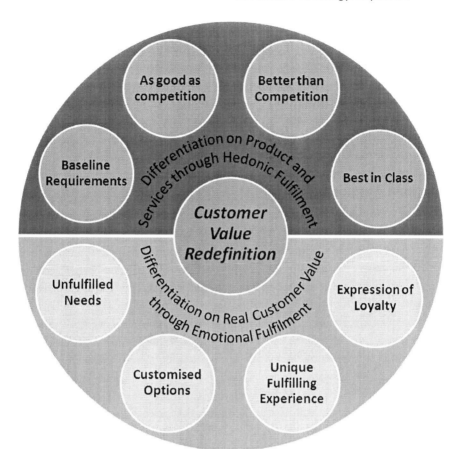

Figure 9 Emotional fulfilment customer differentiation

As the pendulum continues to swing and move towards the customer experience dimension, the concept of co-creation will move from the direct relationship between provider and customer into, as explained previously, customer to customer dialogues and communications. In other words, achieving co-creation brand advocacy strategies means that providers will be encouraged to create networks of partnerships amongst all stakeholders. Furthermore, it means aligning the brand values with the notion of the empowered customer value drive. Having the customer in the driving seat means that the mindset will have to focus on a transparent and trustworthy approach with customers, and the treatment of the customer as a total partner, which is reliable and dependable, and which can be entrusted with taking the brand within the community out there (Figure 10).

Figure 10 Co-creation brand advocacy strategies

The evolution of customer loyalty towards customer intimacy and customer advocacy is based on a continuum, which includes four different levels of relationships and four different stages of maturity. These include the following:

- *Customer engagement and empowerment*: it means moving away towards the 'do it yourself' customer perspective through a focus on customer experience philosophy and adopting a new marketing style which is driven by one to one relationships. This also means that the customer experience can use modern concepts, such as re-imagination to ensure that the fulfilment of design is really to evoke a positive reaction from the emotional perspective.

- *Customer empathy*: it means that as the customer becomes more involved and more empowered, organisations will have to appoint individuals who can advise the customer and to create the mechanism for customer interface, and who can provide the right information and let the customer access the required knowledge resources.

- *Customer value continuum*: it means that customer centric commerce will evolve towards an external perspective where value is perceived as an individual measurement from customer based plans, total loyalty, and ultimately to emotional satisfaction.

- *Customer oriented transformational thinking*: it means moving from the 'customer is king' philosophy towards a philosophy of real customer value, where the customer measures the 'for me only', or 'my own', into how they perceive the fulfilment to have taken place (Figure 11).

Figure 11: Total customer experience management: an integrated model

Excellence Tetralogy: the business element

As discussed previously, the four key elements of the Excellence Tetralogy philosophy mean that the focus of leadership in terms of creating constancy of purpose and stimulating growth will be reflected in turn to show how the businesses focuses on its performance and on delivering its stakeholder impact. A model concept of sustainable business is to ensure that there is a paradigm shift from the traditional model of shareholder orientation towards a new concept of stakeholder orientation. As Figure 12 illustrates, the business element model explains the various components that are necessary for creating a continuum of business growth and development based on an integrated, sustainable approach to delivering growth and development in the short, medium and long term.

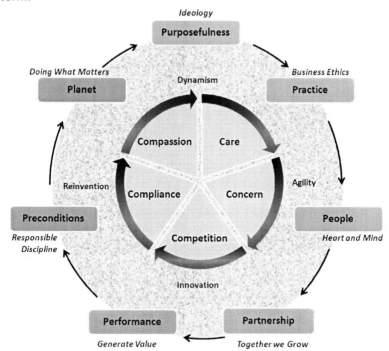

Figure 12: Excellence Tetralogy: the business element

27

The core of the business

The core philosophy of a business and how it wishes to impact is based on the 5Cs principles:

- *Care*: every business will have to have a customer centric or a stakeholder centric approach. It means that it has to deploy all of its resources and capabilities towards the fulfilment of its stakeholders.

- *Concern*: having concern for its people, employees and partners and ensuring that there is nurturing, development, engagement, empowerment, reward and recognition and retention at all levels.

- *Competition*: having a smart approach towards studying competition and developing strategies for ensuring that the capabilities that are deployed will truly deliver either at parity level or above what the competition is doing.

- *Compliance*: ensuring that the organisation operates within the legal frame and compliant with regulations such as Health and Safety, for instance.

- *Compassion*: beyond the traditional model of profit orientation, a sustainable business will operate within the focus on its local community and beyond and having concern for the needs of outside stakeholders.

The structure of the business

The proposition that the structure of a business, as opposed to its core (the 5Cs), is based on the 7Ps approach. These seven elements define the ideology, the practice, the value, the impact and the concern. The 7Ps are more relevant to the 'how' aspect of a business.

- *Purposefulness*: an important element on how a business defines its purpose and deploys its guiding principles in order to ensure continuity and sustainability.

- *Practice*: how businesses define their ethical conduct and ensure that the practice is in tandem with the ideology being practiced.

- *People*: how a business engages the heart and minds of all of its employees.

- *Partnerships*: how a business engages with its suppliers and external partners through a win-win situation and through a philosophy of 'together we grow'.

- *Performance*: how a business intends to generate value from its stakeholders' perspective.

- *Pre-conditions*: how a business operates in a responsible and disciplined manner and does not break the law.

- *Planet*: how a business continues to do what really matters in terms of the ozone layer, emissions, recycling, green issues, committee based projects, etcetera.

The dynamism of the business

The dynamism of a business, as depicted in Figure 12, has to operate similarly to a living cell that replenishes itself through the interface with its external environment. The healthy growth of a living cell is driven by key ingredients, and in the context of a sustainable business there are four nutrients of growth and long term health that need to be taken into account.

- *Dynamism*: ensuring that businesses are flexible and responsive in a dynamic manner so as to ensure they can adapt to changes in the external environment and deploy the right capabilities in the right way for the right impact.

- *Agility*: ensuring that speed of reaction is important, but also ensuring that alertness to opportunities out there is exploited to the full.

- *Innovation*: ensuring that this remains the key source of fuelling effort, value added and effective contribution to all the key stakeholders involved.

- *Re-invention*: ensuring that the sustainable business model continues to evolve and that the open system perspective system suggested allows leadership to make decisions about the re-engineering and re-invention so that the mentality is compatible with model requirements and the mindset is really in tune with what the market requirements are, and what the stakeholders want from the business.

References

Battor, M. (2008) *Capabilities and Business Performance: A Conceptual Model and Empirical Examination in the Financial Services Industry*, University of Bradford, Doctor of Philosophy.

Martinette, L.A., Johnson, W.C. and Obenchain, A. M. (2003) *Market orientation and business process orientation: how they relate to perceived customer value and received shareholder value*, Hawaii International Conference on Business.

Woodruff, R. (1997) Customer Value: the Next Source for Competitive Advantage, *Journal of the Academy of marketing Science*. 25, (2), 139-153.

Further Reading

Excellence Tetralogy – Gutsy Leadership
Leadership in the modern context cannot be distracted from steering the organisations that they are responsible along the path to success, from the point of view of making useful and successful repeated journeys of realising competitive business performance on the one hand, but also the overall health and sustainability of the business has to be maintained for the long term. Leaders will have to use balanced judgment, scientific approaches based on information and analysis of markets, competition, customer feedback etc., and also they have to use cumulative experience on what makes sense and what pleases and delights the customer.

Excellence Tetralogy – Distinctive Capability
Business performance, which is defined as a relative concept, and has to be looked at in the context of sustainable performance and continuity of the business itself, is heavily dependent on a wide variety of orientations that need to be introduced within the business in a systematic way, nurtured and developed in the minds of employees, converted into practices, built in the operating systems and exploited to the full, so as to provide value internally and externally.

Excellence Tetralogy – Inspired Customer

The third element of the Excellence Tetralogy is perhaps the most important element and concerns the evolution of customer mentality and the emergence of the tribal customer. The implications of internet technology has meant that the adoption of the customer centric commerce philosophy has shifted from a drive towards fulfilling the tangible transactional needs of customers and delivering the economics of companies towards focusing on improving the economies of the individuals instead.

Excellence Tetralogy – Sustainable Business

The focus of leadership in terms of creating constancy of purpose and stimulating growth will be reflected in turn to show how the businesses focuses on its performance and on delivering its stakeholder impact. A model concept of sustainable business is to ensure that there is a paradigm shift from the traditional model of shareholder orientation towards a new concept of stakeholder orientation. The business element model explains the various components that are necessary for creating a continuum of business growth and development based on an integrated, sustainable approach to delivering growth and development in the short, medium and long term.

CU00651416

Neuropsychology for Co

Understanding the basics

Coaching in Practice series

The aim of this series is to help coaching professionals gain a broader understanding of the challenges and issues they face in coaching, enabling them to make the leap from being a 'good-enough' coach to an outstanding one. This series is an essential aid for both the novice coach eager to learn how to grow a coaching practice, and the more experienced coach looking for new knowledge and strategies. Combining theory with practice, the series provides a comprehensive guide to becoming successful in this rapidly expanding profession.

Published and forthcoming titles:

Bluckert: *Psychological Dimensions to Executive Coaching*
Brockbank: *Coaching with Empathy*
Brown and Brown: *Neuropsychology for Coaches: understanding the basics*
Driver: *Coaching Positively*
Hawkins: *Creating a Coaching Culture*
Hay: *Reflective Practice and Supervision for Coaches*
Hayes: *NLP Coaching*
Paice: *New Coach: Reflections from a Learning Journey*
Rogers: *Developing a Coaching Business*
Sandler: *Executive Coaching: A Psychodynamic Approach*
Vaughan Smith: *Therapist into Coach*
Wildflower: *The Hidden History of Coaching*

Neuropsychology for Coaches

Understanding the basics

Professor Paul Brown and Virginia Brown

Open University Press

Open University Press
McGraw-Hill Education
McGraw-Hill House
Shoppenhangers Road
Maidenhead
Berkshire
England
SL6 2QL

email: enquiries@openup.co.uk
world wide web: www.openup.co.uk

and Two Penn Plaza, New York, NY 10121–2289, USA

First published 2012

A catalogue record of this book is available from the British Library

ISBN-13: 978-0-33-524547-5 (pb)
ISBN-10: 0-33-524547-1 (pb)
eISBN: 978-0-33-524548-2

Library of Congress Cataloging-in-Publication Data
CIP data applied for

Typesetting and e-book compilations by
RefineCatch Limited, Bungay, Suffolk
Printed and bound by CPI Group (UK) Ltd, Croydon, CR0 4YY

Fictitious names of companies, products, people, characters and/or data that may be used herein (in case studies or in examples) are not intended to represent any real individual, company, product or event.

"It's rare to find an accessible, engaging book that combines current neuropsychological theory with working examples for executive coaching. At last here is one that brings the two together seamlessly. Well written and informative, the authors delight the reader from the first to the last page, creating rich pictures through metaphor, case studies and highly practical models. Their emphasis on the importance of trust in enabling change and development within the coaching relationship is particularly welcome in these often reductionist times. And their curiosity and wonder is catching – they do not profess to know all the answers, but give us much food for thought about our own coaching practice. This book gives coaches (and in fact anyone involved in people development) a thorough grounding in this increasingly important subject; it really is a must-read for new or experienced coaches alike, and one which I think rightly deserves to become a classic text."

Linda Aspey, Managing Director, Coaching for Leaders

"At last, a book that embeds the practice of coaching into what we know of how the brain works – rather than one that tells you about the brain, then leaves the coach to work it out; or one that tells you about techniques, then adds in the brain information as something of a 'P.S'.

This book works at many levels: whether for the coach with a fresh curiosity about the neuroscience, or one already using some knowledge to inform their practice, all the fundamentals are there, in a style that avoids over-simplifying, yet makes the complex accessible and 'ready to use'. This is a gem of a resource for the coach who wants to take their practice beyond technique into robust knowledge and understanding of what's going on in the client's brain, the coach's brain and, indeed, between the two brains as they interact. It helps us to understand why what works, works; and what might be happening when what we expect to work simply doesn't."

Ann James, Executive Coach / Director, Thinking Space

"At long last, a rigorous book on neuropsychology that is both palatable and practically applicable for executive coaches. I like the way it develops an approach starting from the way the brain works rather than adding in information about the brain to the way the coach works. There has been so much demand for a relevant knowledge base around neuroscience, and I think that most coaches will find this book an invaluable source and aide memoire."

Dr Tara Swart, Neuroscientist, medical doctor and executive coach, Executive Performance Ltd.

PB says:
To Tom, in gratitude,
and from whom I go on learning
more than he will ever know and who
found Laos and so Vone, Katie and JJ.

VB says:
To my family, who are at the heart of everything

Contents

Series Editor's Preface

For most of its short history, coaching has been a discipline where intelligent speculation and research about what works and what doesn't has been confined to the social and psychological sciences. Now a new discipline has entered the field: neuroscience. That is the subject of this welcome and urgently needed book.

Neuroscience will, for certain, revolutionize coaching. For the first time we have the opportunity to understand at least a little about the biological basis of our behaviour and that includes the behaviour of the coach as well as of the client. The authors of this book emphasize throughout that we are merely at the beginning of understand the workings of the human brain, but even so, what we already know is enough to challenge many of the myths and half truths that both we and our clients may believe – for instance that feelings are a side issue and that all our decisions are made on the basis of rationality.

Neuroscience is a sprawling and potentially overwhelming area and much of the writing about it, welcome though it is, is produced for other scientists. This is daunting for coaches, especially for those of us who left science behind at school. In this book the authors start from easily-understood basic brain functioning and then go on to explain how we can use this knowledge to enrich our coaching and make it incomparably more effective.

It is not an option to ignore this fascinating new area of insight into human functioning and I commend this book to you as a friendly, authoritative guide as to how to incorporate the intriguing findings of current neuroscience into your daily practice as a coach. The authors combine deep knowledge of the biological and psychological science with many years of wisdom and experience as coaches themselves.

Jenny Rogers
Series Editor

Preface

Paul says:

Virginia and I met at a NeuroGroup I was running that Jane Meyler, of Meyler Coaching, had provoked into existence. Executive coaches had come for six monthly sessions to find out how the brain sciences might contribute to their coaching practice. Virginia said she would like to see how we could develop a pack of materials that would be useful for coaches who had no real knowledge of the way the brain worked but knew they needed to know. Despite being a surname in widespread use, it happened that for more than fifty years I had never come across anyone else called Brown outside my own family, and that seemed as good a reason as any to share our joint enthusiasm for the brain and start doing something together.

Then, serendipitously, Jenny Rogers as Series Editor for McGraw Hill/ Open University asked for a book on how the brain sciences might be used in executive coaching. Nothing could have been better timed. The delivery date was to be a month before I planned to go and live and work in Lao PDR hoping, at the Lao Government's request, to apply the neurosciences for the long-term benefit of a poor but vibrant country that was becoming increasingly market-led. So we abandoned the knowledge pack and set about the book, with McGraw Hill/OU's gentle encouragement in the shape of Jenny and Dr Monika Lee, abetted by the invaluable firm timetable discipline of Richard Townrow.

What we hope to have done, at a very early moment in the development of the neurosciences, is to set out a framework within which an executive coach might systematically start to use the immense power of the knowledge that is pouring out of neuroscience research labs worldwide. In doing so we have synthesized what we as working coaches think is useful in practice. What we have especially *not* wanted to do is simply swamp a prospective user with facts about the wonders of the brain without any overall way of using those facts, or giving a sense that what a good coach should be doing is blinding people with science. In doing this we have relied more on the integrating models based on attachment theory that are coming from the interpersonal neurobiologists, of which Dan Siegel at UCLA is the main proponent, rather than on the detailed localization laboratory work of the large army of cognitive social neuroscientists who have that extraordinary piece of equipment, the fMRI scanner, at their command.

When, in early 2012, there was a conference in New York that attracted over thirty thousand neuroscientists to its deliberations, we were confirmed in our belief that an integrating approach rather than a research-detailed approach might be most helpful to executive coaches. An integrating approach will, if it is on the right tracks, permit the slow accretion of relevant information by which any model and working practices may be strengthened.

Executive coaches are generally a pragmatic bunch of people who find themselves in a rather extraordinary position that we think they do not always appreciate. They are the only people in the corporate world who have regular one-on-one encounters with some of the most interesting, senior and demanding individuals in that world without there being any presumption of illness, distress or disorder in creating the coaching encounter: just a great demand from clients to grow, perform better, and develop their own resources in their own and their firms' interests. We have also observed that, while executive coaches are fascinated by the human condition but have little knowledge of the brain, neuroscientists have a great fascination with the brain but, professionally, not much interest in the human condition. Our task has been to try to bridge that gap. To the extent that we have, readers will be the judge.

The case material contained here is all true but is sufficiently disguised in essential details for the individuals to be composite. We, of course, have learnt most of what we have hoped to impart here from working with clients. Our intention in our own work is always to start with trying to understand what the brain of the client is saying to us, and leave to one side how anything we have thought in the past might have made us start from how we thought it ought to be. That is the challenge for coaches through the second decade of the twenty-first century if they are to develop a real profession underpinned by knowledge at the forward edge of science. To paraphrase William Morris, have only in your own mind what you know to be true about the brain, we beg you, and find your own best way of using what you know. In becoming a brain-to-brain coach leave twentieth-century systems behind, or stress test them by what you increasingly know. In the service of our clients we executive coaches have the opportunity to enter a new world of understanding human behaviour using the brain sciences as a guide.

* * *

How to *write* about excitement?

It's one of the challenges we have set ourselves in structuring a book for coaches about using the basics of the brain. Also, how about trust and love and fear and anger and more tough stuff besides? They are the essence of the way your brain works. This book is about the newly-emerging story of why as people we are the way we are; and how you as an executive coach can use that knowledge. It looks through the lens of the modern neurosciences and asks what the implications of that are for your professional work.

Our own story in getting to write this book starts by accident. No, not so much accident as coincidence, or perhaps synchronicity, or even as evidence of the existence of parallel universes in an utterly quantum fashion.

The elements are these.

In 1996 Daniel Goleman published *Emotional Intelligence*. A raw and difficult and in some ways quite confused and confusing book, it nevertheless signalled a real shift in the way we could understand emotions and, most importantly, it brought emotions into corporate awareness.

Quite separately, through the middle 1990s, British Telecom had been running a series of television advertisements around their strap-line – 'It's good to talk'. That phrase has sunk into British consciousness. In a series of advertisements Bob Hoskins and Maureen Lipman acted out brief family dramas on the telephone involving absent children that, nearly twenty years later, people still smile about.

The then Head of Telephones at BT began to wonder what the wider marketing and social implications of this powerful phrase might mean for the business as a whole. He asked Alan (now Lord) Watson of the corporate communications agency Burson Marsteller to think imaginatively about how to explore that thought. Alan Watson went to talk to Joanna Foster, the then recent Chair of the Equal Opportunities Commission and previous Head of the Pepperell Unit at the Industrial Society. She was given a brief to create a small team of consultants to actively explore what the wider social implications of 'It's good to talk' might mean. PB had the good fortune to be part of that team and found himself on a two-year part-time attachment to BT.

It so happened that VB was working for BT global sales at the time. PB and VB did not actually meet until fifteen years later, and though they share a common surname are not related in any way at all except through a fascination with brain and behaviour and this book. Through quite separate routes they both became executive coaches, and met in 2007 when VB joined a series of NeuroGroup seminars for executive coaches that PB had started. The seminars were about how the brain works and the way the modern neurosciences were giving us insights of an entirely new kind into understanding executive behaviour.

In the work that Joanna Foster inspired at BT there was an opportunity to invite Daniel Goleman to London for the first public presentation about emotional intelligence in the UK. He was the keynote speaker at a great one-day conference where, based on his work, PB's presentation redefined Descartes' dictum 'Cogito ergo sum – I think, therefore I am'. It became 'Cogito sentioque ergo sum – I think and feel, therefore I am'. A colleague, Brenda Hales, has recently said it could be put more elegantly as : 'I feel and therefore think I am'. That's good.

VB attended that conference but we didn't find out she had done so until we started writing this book. Nor, specifically, and to his cheerful chagrin, did she remember PB's redefinition of Descartes' dictum. But she did recall a sense that she was left with from the conference that something was changing in the world. To her surprise she is now part of making that manifest with this book. Which is where synchronicity leads one to places that one could never have imagined but that retrospectively have a clear inevitability about them. PB and Alan Watson were also at the same school, but that was complete coincidence.

Over the past fifteen years brain-imaging technology has been developing remarkably. When PB was first a clinical student at the Maudsley Hospital's Institute of Psychiatry in London fifty years ago it seemed remarkable that brain waves could be tracked through scalp electrodes via an electroencephalograph (EEG) machine; and that disturbances in brain waves could be linked to evidence of psychological impairments demonstrated through psychological testing.

Nowadays, brain scanning via magnetic resonance imaging (MRI and fMRI) produces an extraordinary sense of being able to see fine cross-sections of the workings of the living brain. And a new imaging technique called Diffusion Tensor Imaging (DTI) is just beginning to show how oxygen molecules flow through brain pathways. As the molecules are tracked, the complex connectivity of the brain in the whole of the cortical system is beginning to be revealed. Even more recently remarkable pictures of the interconnectedness of brain cells through a technique called functional connectomy are making the specifics even more apparent. They show what looks like the wiring diagram of the brain.

So these are intensely exciting times for the brain sciences. Real laboratory knowledge about how the brain works is beginning to replace twentieth-century psychological theorizing and speculation. It may well be that within twenty years psychology as a discipline disappears altogether and neurobiology coupled with a resurgence in ethics and morality become the basic disciplines for creating an account of why human beings behave the way they do.

But that's getting speculative. To be contentious instead, think as a coach of the fact that the organizational application of the neurosciences is up for grabs. As an emerging profession, executive coaches have a rare opportunity to become knowledge-based professionals rather than the practice-and-technique-based professionals that they currently are. With the great privilege they have of spending one-on-one time with some of the most interesting and effective people in the corporate world, to our minds that is a prize that is worth a serious amount of effort. It would keep executive coaching at the forefront of individual and organizational effectiveness and, most importantly of all, serve the executive client very well indeed.

So this book is about the excitement of getting to that place.

The brain is the most complex bit of kit in the known universe. Every one of us has a brain that is essentially similar to every other brain on the planet and yet completely unique. Its job is to regulate your bodily systems, manage your emotions, attach emotions to events perceived by the five senses to create meaning, and thereby make each of us the person that we are. Oh, and to do this seamlessly so that, to the outside, we each appear integrated. In doing this it uses the entirely private database of your own experience and is especially attracted and responsive to anything to do with relationship. It makes sense of you as the reference point for making sense of the world in which you have an 'I' and a 'me' and, to others, are an 'other'. If it can't make good sense *of* you it can't make good sense *for* you.

Although we come into the world with five senses, we have no specific sense for making sense of other people who, in their turn, are making sense of us. The fluid nature of such an arrangement requires the brain to try to find certainties, and it can do this in a rigid, chaotic or fairly flexible manner. The way it was trained from the first day of life – perhaps from the fourth month of gestation, actually – essentially defines how it will work. But it is always relationship that defines its existence – relationship if not with another person then certainly with itself. If that sounds circular, it is. For the brain constructs its Self which in turn shapes the brain so that, unlike all other animals, with whom we human beings share consciousness, only human beings are self-conscious.

A question we have left entirely to one side throughout the book is the question of whether there is any difference between the male and female brain. The answer is, there is: profoundly so. But the subtleties of the differences do not contradict the underlying structure of this book, which is concerned with understanding enough about the brain to use that knowledge in practice. As you learn to listen to the brain you will start enquiring for yourself about male and female differences, and then perhaps marvel that we are so different and yet so much the same.

This is, we believe, the first book to attempt to define the practice of coaching from what we know about the brain rather than use what we know about the brain to justify bits of coaching; as if bits of knowledge about the brain were like specially good fairy lights on a Christmas tree, shining when hung out to view but of only passing significance. We know that it is work in progress from working coaches. In presenting it we hope it will let other working coaches begin to sense how they might shift their practice to a brain-based point of view: and in doing so join in at the beginning of a voyage of discovery that for everyone is new.

Paul Brown   *Virginia Brown*
National Science Council, Vientiane, Lao PDR   *Hitchin, Herts., UK*

1 Biographical beginnings
Making sense of the brain

Introduction

This chapter builds a picture of how your brain is working at trying to understand how your client's brain is working and how, in consequence, you understand the person you are coaching. Your brain is a social brain. The first fundamental proposition for the whole book is that

> *your brain is the organ that evolved to make sense to others of the way you make sense of yourself.*

We are all unique

The neurosciences of the last fifteen years now leave no doubt at all that everything you do, think or feel at any moment of the day or night has a complex **neurochemistry** attached to it. That neurochemistry is created by your experience, determines your behaviour, and constructs the essence of the person that you are.

If it is your own individual chemistry that makes you unique the same is true for the client you coach. So how might it be best to understand that uniqueness? In the way that all artists use similar raw materials to create something entirely unlike anything else in the world, so (unless you are an identical twin) you have been fashioned out of the raw materials to hand into something entirely unlike anybody else – though the raw materials start out being much like everyone else's. Procreation provides the raw materials. Life provides the shape they take. Human life is, at root, the complex interplay of the neurochemistry in our brain triggered by the infinite stimuli of experience and then arranged by the functioning of the brain.

Not many books about brains mention bricks. But, like brain cells, they are basic to the structures in which – at least in the Western world – we function for much of our lives; and they are more familiar than brain cells. To get you thinking about something unfamiliar, like brain cells, let's start with something familiar. Try this analogy.

Imagine an enormous pile of bricks and what could be constructed from them. As part of the background structure of your everyday life bricks – like brain cells – may hold no special fascination for you. Without a specific interest (laying a garden path: building an extension to your house), it is likely that you have rarely had cause to inspect *bricks* as such. Nevertheless you may have strong views about buildings – perhaps when you visit one whose beauty takes your breath away; and not least of all when you mortgage your future to buy a house, when you will certainly want the bricks to be in good shape and sound.

Think of the key people in your life – the person that you married, live with, coach, see developing in your children, worry about in an ageing parent, your boss. The way the brain cells of all those key people in your life have been organized defines each of them as the person that each one is or has been in relationship to you. Learning how to read the way they have been organized is the best way of getting inside other people's heads and looking at the world through their eyes. When you can do that you can start to coach with a skill that is beyond the social skills and organizational experience that have already made you as effective a coach as you are.

Building blocks of the brain

To push the analogy, the bricks that made one house might have made any other. The same pile of bricks could make the meanest row of standardized housing or the most beautiful Georgian building. Yet an invitation to go into a mean-looking house might surprise you with the warmth and welcome and even beauty of its interior; whilst an invitation into the Georgian house might leave you puzzled by the coldness, blocked-off rooms and sense of shabbiness there. It's much the same meeting a person.

Someone – a builder, architect, bricklayer, interior designer and decorator – made all the decisions and did the work that affects the way the building looks. Within the limitations of what bricks can do the possibilities are huge.

So it is with people. Within the broad options of how the brain organizes itself, individuality is a function of the way the brain got itself organized. Parents, through their genes, commission the design. Mother is the architect. Parental add-ons – teachers, peer groups and teenage idols, to name but three – are project managers and interior decorators in the brain-to-person organizing process. Fathers hold the special place of strengthening what mothers start.

The developing brain

As we humans grow and become increasingly independent we each acquire, to a greater or lesser extent, the capacity to do some of our own interior decoration and design. We create our own internal world. Teenagers try that out physically too – in attic bedrooms with lurid colours on the walls, or the posters they choose that are special to them. So the Self that we project to others is a compound of the way others shaped us and, bit by bit, our Self grows to the point where it can take on the task for its Self.

The eighty billion brain cells that any one of us has when we come into the world have evolved to have a huge amount of potential. But early on in life – and beyond the survival reflexes like crying, sucking, coughing, sneezing, sleeping, waking and being able to get rid of bodily waste – they have no ordered connecting structure of the pathways that are created out of experience: just enormous potential.

What makes that potential effective is the capacity of the brain to start ordering itself in response to the data it receives from the sense organs that our genes have supplied us with – touch, taste, sight, smell and hearing. The brain of an infant is hungry for the stimulation of its senses – but in an ordered manner. It cannot make sense of too much at once – at least, not until it has begun to learn how to manage too much at once.

The self-organizing brain

The brain does not come into the world with a template as to how everything should be. The parts of the brain that organize the automatic background to life – heart rate, salt levels, waking, sleeping, breathing, digestion, elimination and everything else that is unknown to us most of the time in the physical background of our existence – are functioning on arrival in the world. But the rest is huge potential. It is life experience – and especially the way we are cared for in the first place – that provides the way the individual's brain gets organized and a unique Self starts developing.

Take one simple example. Any child at birth can learn any one of the more-than five thousand languages that are spoken in the world. Which one a child will learn is entirely an accident of conception, hearing the rhythms of that language whilst in a mother's womb, and beginning to use it as the power of speech slowly develops in the relationships of the first year of life and the power of language develops increasingly in the next two.

Before the age of three an infant can learn two or even three and perhaps even more languages without the least understanding that they are different and without the least difficulty. John Stuart Mill was fluent in classical Greek by the age of three. The brain develops according to the experience it is offered. It is only later that learning a new language becomes complicated by the awareness that you are learning a new language: and by the fact that networks have already been established for the first language learnt that make it easier to maintain that language than create new pathways for a different one.

Language is enormously influential in shaping you. The language you first learn starts to define you, create your view of the world you live in and your own view of your Self and those around you. But it might have been any one of those more than five thousand options that would have created other pathways in your brain – though all the pathways for whatever language would have used the centres of the brain especially devoted to language.

But specialized centres are no use without them being connected together. This is the great puzzle for understanding the brain. The brain is organized to have various parts of it responsive to each of the five senses plus muscular control. And they appear to be highly differentiated centres, scattered throughout the brain. How then are each of the differentiated centres integrated so that they work seamlessly as a whole? We could ask the same question of complex organizations. How does each major department work but, more importantly, how well and effectively do they all work together?

Your clients' brains

So the starting point for making sense of the person you coach is an under-standing that individuality comes from life experience moulding the genetic potential from which it all started. Life experience shapes the brain through the neurochemistry that experience generates. And the neurochemistry is made active through the cellular electrical activity that makes the brain live. The interesting questions for a coach are: How? What happened? What made this person the person that they are? Getting the answer to those and similar questions opens up the possibility of finding a way into understanding the person. The answers lie in understanding the way the brain of your client – and your brain too – got organized.

Relationship that shapes the brain

A certain answer to approaching these questions has only become apparent recently. The way your brain gets organized is entirely to do with relationships. The task of the growing brain is to get itself well-activated through relationship which, through various iterations, takes the first twenty-four years of life.

But first of all to become effective the brain has to learn how to manage itself. Making that happen is the key parental task and, the evidence now shows, it is especially a mother's task. It is not that a father or another carer will not do. It is just that a mother seems to have special power to do it especially well.

Professional wisdom through most of the twentieth century, and going back to the Greeks, thought that a baby arrived in the world as a blank slate – Aristotle's *tabula rasa* – ready for life's experiences to be recorded. But it is now known that from month four of foetal life a baby's brain *in utero* is subject to the biochemical influences of a mother's experiences. We all come into the world with a brain already primed for the world that our mother has been experiencing.

A father's key job seems to be to strengthen the connections that the mother initiates. If a mother is the architect a father is like the structural engineer. Both have an intensely important job to do before the child becomes self-sustaining – finding his or her own strengths and becoming his or her own person through gradually taking increasing control of managing the interior decorating too.

What the infant brain needs to get it working well is to be structured and organized by another functioning brain. That is a huge statement. From it comes the key principle that operates throughout the rest of our lives and it depends upon the quality of relationship. In organizations, relationship is the essence of good leadership and of being well led. It is the life-blood of any organization. And it is vitally true for effective coaching. What a client's brain needs to get it moving in the direction for which the coaching contract has been established, therefore, is to be organized by another functioning brain within the context of an effective relationship. It is through relationship that the brain is made live to the possibility of change.

The coaching relationship

By 'effective coaching' from a brain-based perspective we mean

> *the capacity of a professional coach to so understand and manage the brain processes of the person who is being coached that effective change and development within that person, plus the consolidation of change and development, is deliberately created and consolidated for that person's benefit, bounded by what has been agreed contractually between the two people involved.*

If, as a coach, you are going to understand your client's brain, and the brain is the organ of relationship that relies on its capacity to make sense of the world, then understanding what is happening in your own brain is a precursor to understanding and, for the purposes of the professional encounter, managing the brain of the person you coach.

Managing the brain of the person you coach is what you are doing in any event when you are coaching. There is, as it happens, no other means of interacting professionally with another person. It can be done accidentally or it can be done by design. In either case it might be done well or done badly. But the chances of doing it well by design seem to be the more likely route to soundly structured professionalism.

Management thinking over the past half century has focused on some aspects of this without having had any of the modern working knowledge of the brain. That is the way knowledge accumulates. Truths develop pragmatically in a way that can only later be tested against greater empirical knowledge.

Using knowledge of the brain

Becoming conscious of eye-contact, body posture, and the possibility of mirroring the other person's gestures, for instance, have all been aspects of management interest without any specific linkage to an integrated understanding of the workings of the brain. Neuro-linguistic programming (NLP) is intrigued by the way observable eye-movement in clients reflects the way they are accessing different parts of the brain and makes a variety of inferences as to what might be happening within the brain as a consequence of observed eye function. People trained in gestalt approaches have similarly made many interesting observations about the meaning of various aspects of social interplay without having been able to have any informed reference to brain function.

In the absence of real knowledge about the workings of the brain, people – executive coaches among them – got on with life. And still do. They did the same before gravity was understood. It was well known before Newton that when working up on a roof a builder was substantially more at risk of falling down than falling up. But it is doubtful if flying would have become possible without some formal understanding of gravity. Even so it took two-hundred-and-fifty years from Newton's insights to the Wright brothers' capacity to get a heavier-than-air contraption off the ground. And it needed the parallel introduction of the petrol engine to provide the motive power – a discovery nothing to do with gravity though profoundly facilitated by the revolution in thinking that Newton and the seventeenth-century emerging sciences started.

Similarly in the modern world social and professional encounters operate without most people involved having any detailed knowledge of the working of the brain behind the encounter. Outside coaching and therapy, perhaps only advertising companies, computer game makers, actors and stand-up comedians think consciously about what might be going on in the brains of their audience as they endeavour to create the effect that they want across the screen or the footlights. At this start of a new age of understanding, though, what some knowledge of the way the brain works will let you do is to do your coaching more by design, more efficiently and, to the extent that both those capacities increase your effectiveness, more professionally.

Social and environmental influences

The brain has its own biography. It grows and matures and decays, sometimes painfully so. The person who is the person with the brain they have is the person they are because of the brain they have. The brain sciences are now certain that there can be no other basis for who the person is.

But at the same time we cannot help but know that we are profoundly affected by those around us. To a not-insubstantial extent we are also the product of the people with whom we interact. That seems contradictory – that we should be both the brain-and-person that we each are and yet be subject to the influences of those around us. But as *The Huffington Post* reported in April 2011, ('Keep your thumbs still when I'm talking to you'):

> The rudeness of texting during a conversation is but one of the new don'ts emerging in the unfolding universe of webequette, the new rules for social life on the web.
>
> But while such pointers may smooth over some trouble spots, they do nothing about the fundamental collision between the ways we connect digitally, and the connections our brain was designed to crave.
>
> Nature designed the brain for face-to-face interactions – not the online world. A new field, social neuroscience, has discovered that large zones of the brain's frontal areas are dedicated to tuning in to the person we're with, picking up their emotions, movement, even intentions, and coordinating what we do with all that.
>
> We have what amounts to a neural WiFi which makes a brain-to-brain bridge while we interact, that operates instantly, unconsciously and powerfully to keep it all going smoothly. More important, when we feel rapport, or come away from a conversation with a friend glowing from a good talk, this is the circuitry that makes us feel that glow.
>
> So what's the problem? The online universe, from Facebook and Twitter to texting to email, has no channel for this vital brain-to-brain flow. All that dialogue seems, well, thin, compared to the richness of actually being with the other person. For the social brain, hundreds of contacts online in a day pale in comparison to a hug.

So the brain makes sense in the context of relationship with others and with its own Self. From earliest days of life the sense we make of the tone of what we hear, how we look and understand how we are looked at, the posture we adopt, the smile or frown that we see and show, are all the result of electrochemical activity in the brain which will have been shaped by encounters with the grown-up brains around us that begin to shape our expectation of the world.

So the essential skill of coaching from a brain perspective is facilitating change in a client in such a way as to get the brain working with new pathways in order to establish and maintain new ways of being. The key to that is relationship backed up by the carrier signals of communication. This is the way in which the brain of your client is enabled to make new sense.

The impact of trauma

Of course circumstances can arise in which the brain hasn't had a chance to tell our body how to be. Traumatic experiences are of such a kind. It is because a traumatic event completely subverts the proper order of events that the brain finds traumatic experiences so hard to process and make sense of.

Tom

Tom was a chartered surveyor, walking around the growing structure on a commercial site of which he was in charge as clerk of works and where there was a great deal of activity. Despite the apparent confusion his trained eye could see that things seemed to be in order for the complexity of interlinked jobs that were in hand.

The next thing Tom knew was waking up in an emergency ward in great pain and heavily bandaged. What he discovered had happened to him was that a sack of cement that had been hoisted up through a fourth floor window had been left balanced on an open sill instead of being taken inside on to the floor. A workman inside the building, manoeuvring a long piece of timber, had inadvertently stubbed the end of the timber that was behind his line of sight into the bag, knocking it out of the window as Tom was walking underneath. It had landed on the back of Tom's head from nearly forty feet high, smashing him face forward on to the ground with his head crashing into a scaffold pole on the way. Tom could ruefully see this was a good cause of his being in hospital.

But that knowledge didn't help. Although Tom recovered physically over the following months he developed a persistent anxiety at the thought of returning to work and began to show the classic symptoms of post-traumatic stress disorder. His attempts to get back on to site produced panic attacks when he was putting on working gear; and when he had actually revisited the scene of the accident he felt a great sense of being detached from his surroundings, felt as if it wasn't him who was there, and broke out into copious sweating. He felt weak to the extent he had nearly fainted. His brain was saying: *Here are unknown dangers. Get out one way or another.*

For a man who had felt proud of his professional skills, had been highly valued for being a practical surveyor good at dealing with tradesmen, and who wanted to support his family, the sense he had of being out of control of himself when contemplating a return to work was immensely troubling. He began to ruminate about his difficulties, started to feel a failure within his marriage, complained of having nothing to live for and wondered about suicide.

Tom's brain was trying to make sense of his experience by running scenarios in his head for which he had no reference points because the experience he had had made no sense to him. The site should not have had such a flagrant breach of safety rules, and the fact that it had and he had been the unfortunate victim of the breach troubled him enormously. In some ways he felt it was right he should have been the victim if things were that bad on his watch.

It is not difficult to see the circular patterns of ungrounded thought that can happen in such circumstances and the way the brain tries to make sense from within the person's own experience when it hasn't been able to process that experience. The advice of well-meaning relatives and friends to forget it and get on with life, to be grateful for the fact he was alive and had made a physical recovery, didn't get into the parts of the brain where the real action was taking place, even though Tom could superficially agree with the advice and want to take it.

The real action was taking place within the **emotional system**. Tom's brain was being flooded with circulating sadness, disgust with his own professional performance on site, shame at what he saw as his own current weakness, and fear of something untoward happening again. He felt unmanned. No amount of trying to redirect himself or accepting the well-meant advice of others was going to shape or change his brain's certainty of the way things were.

This type of reaction to a completely unforeseen event is not at all uncommon. When something happens that makes no sense – is non-sense – so far as the brain is concerned, the brain does not know how to process it. And it is difficult to make sense retrospectively of strongly-established non-sense. That is because sense is only made through feeling and fact being attached to each other in a time sequence. That is how the brain creates meaning that can then be attached to words – though it is not an uncommon experience that the meaning of something may be so profound that words are not adequate to its description.

Fear

A post-traumatic reaction occurs when the brain starts triggering intense fear reactions when it has not had the chance to locate them within a proper logging of the event. So it triggers fear reactions to inappropriate events 'just in case'. Once that reaction has happened it becomes a new circuit of fear in the brain, because the brain itself cannot distinguish between what is objectively true and what is not. That is the function of reason. When meaning at the time of the event has been bypassed the brain can only work on what it has actually experienced. If the processes of reason got bypassed then the brain can only work 'un-reasonably'. This does not mean that the brain is working irrationally. It will, from a brain's perspective, be working logically within the way the brain works. But it may nevertheless be confused about what is objectively true and what is not.

The difficulty of being different

The best bet for the brain is always to trust its own experience. It is this that makes change so difficult for change, by definition, carries the presumption that the person is going somewhere new. That may be intellectually exciting and challenging but, to the brain, that spells danger more than opportunity. And so intention to be different does not easily get translated into actions that are different. The best bet, for the brain, is always to go on being the same. 'The brain that got me here is the one most likely to get me there', says the brain to itself. It is a conundrum to which we shall keep returning.

Non-sense seems to happen remarkably frequently in many organizations. It is not so immediately dramatic as a bag of cement from four storeys high but the brain, if it cannot make good sense of what is happening, will make the best sense it can. And often that is to consign what is happening to the 'nonsense' bin and have nothing more to do with it.

Consider a department going through a period of reorganization or restructuring. Whilst efforts may have been made to articulate the rationale for the impending changes, what is experienced by the individuals facing such uncertainty is strongly driven by a **threat response** triggered by their brain. Working with clients in such situations we notice that the threat response impacts, for example, their ability to think clearly and to maintain a broader perspective. Even though an individual might try to set aside all thoughts of uncertainty and get on with his job, his brain will not let him maintain its rational focus for the emotional brain has its own rationality that, as part of the rule structure of the brain, overrides the thinking brain. As Pascal said in another context: 'The heart has its reasons of which reason has no understanding'.

From an observer's point of view, of course, nonsense can take many forms. One of them creates laughter. It is the basis of all slapstick film comedy – though the participants never laugh. The brain experiencing nonsense doesn't like it. For the person to whom the 'non-sense' happens the brain is left with the task of processing something that has no meaning and the brain hates that state of affairs.

The three parts of the brain

The brain consists of three main parts. Together they form the **'triune' brain**. They come from three stages of our evolutionary history. Although not all neuroscientists agree with this evolutionary theory it has a clarity and usefulness about it that has not been bettered by any other view. And being, as you are, at the coal face of wanting to know enough to be of use to your client, this three-part view of the brain will serve you well until something better comes along.

The Reptilian Brain

Reptiles are massively older than humans in the evolutionary record. They had brains long before us. But only reptilian brains.

Think of a snake with a long spinal column down its sinuous body. At the head-end of the spinal column, protected by the bony helmet of the skull, is a small brain that regulates everything that the snake needs to do instinctively and reflexively. You have that kind of 'snake brain'. At the top of your spine is a part of the brain that regulates everything that keeps the body going automatically – breathing, heart rate, salt levels, and so on. It is the part of the brain that is functioning when a baby at full term comes into the world with all the sneezing, crying, coughing, sleeping, yawning, waking, eliminating and many other reflexes functioning. It is also the part of the brain that persists in fighting for life when a person is technically 'brain dead'. When all consciousness and the capacity to make sense of the world has gone or been damaged beyond repair, the oldest part of the brain will do its best to stay just ticking over keeping the basic bodily functions just going. We become most aware of the snake brain when it goes wrong.

The Mammalian Brain

About the time the dinosaurs died out a new kind of creature appears in the fossil record. Unlike the egg-laying reptiles, this creature produced live young and started the whole group of creatures that we class as mammals. In basic biology everyone is taught that the special thing about mammals is that they produce live young.

And that is true. But what had passed biologists by – and until recently, from an evolutionary point of view, most psychologists – is that it was a consequence of live young appearing that the live young needed care; which needed a new kind of brain. So a new part of the brain started to appear that had the special capacity to manage relationship. That part of the brain – the second part in evolutionary terms of the three-part brain – is called the **limbic system**. It contains a specially concentrated clustering of **nerve cells**, divided into two parts, one in each half of the brain, called the **amygdala**. The amygdala can both receive and send emotional signals of all kinds, which is what makes managing relationships possible. The limbic system is especially the '**mammalian brain**'.

The Cognitive Brain

And then in remarkably recent time, from an evolutionary point of view, a third part of the brain developed on top of the limbic system. This is the outer part of the brain that in its folds and fissures looks like a walnut and, just like a walnut, is divided into two halves. This is the new brain – the **neocortex** or the '**cognitive brain**' – busy receiving signals from the other two parts of the brain and, from within its own complex pathways, integrating them into a composite whole. It is the part of the brain that is making sense of the world both 'out there' and 'in here'. All other life forms have some kind of consciousness but, so far as is known, only human beings have self-consciousness – the capacity of the brain to organize itself around a representation to itself of its Self.

The cognitive brain integrates the entire working of the brain into a functioning single system and, through the medium of language, tries to make conscious sense of experience. The extent to which it is successful in making sense seems to define the capability of the individual. The better the sense-maker, the more capable – though there is a huge contextual element to this too that will be revisited later.

Whole brain system – synaptic connections

The whole brain system is infinitely more complex than anything yet devised by human beings. In somewhat less than four pounds of brain there are eighty billion brain cells **synaptically** interconnected by several thousand miles of nerve cells operating in a hundred known **chemical regulating agents**, supported by miles of miniscule blood vessels and untold mysteries of how, almost flawlessly, all these components work together. The brain is referred to very readily these days, as being 'hard-wired'. In being human there is remarkably little that is hard-wired in the way that the motherboard of your computer is certainly hard-wired and all soldered together.

But brain cells do need to connect to each other to form networks. A cell may be as small as the width of a hair or over two metres long. Each cell has a varying number of slender sinuous branches coming from it, called **axons** and **dendrites**. Cells connect to each other through the branching of an axon connecting to a dendrite of another cell. On average there are ten thousand possible connections for any one cell to other cells. But attaching happens not by making a physical link but by making a neurochemical connection.

Making connections

Between each axon/dendrite connection is a miniscule gap called a **synaptic gap**. What passes from one cell to another across the gap are molecules stimulated by an electrical charge flowing down the axon to its tip where the chemicals are stored. This charge can flow in only one direction, and it makes it possible for the neurochemical that encodes the information travelling across the gap into the dendrite to trigger (technically '**excite**') the next cell and so on and so on. In such ways are networks formed. The more the same pathway is triggered the more certain does it become that it will be more easily triggered again. And the stronger the stimulus is that starts the charge the more certainly and for longer will the nerve cells – **neurons** – fire. In this way repeated experience creates networked pathways and makes us creatures of habit. The cells that fire together wire together. That is the way the brain organizes itself.

To illustrate, think of all the children in a school – say a thousand of them – milling around the playground. Ask one child to start a chain so that everyone in the playground joins hands to two other children so that the whole school is networked together except that the children at each end of the network have only one connection. Then ask them to hold their hands so that palms are facing each other but not quite touching. Every child represents a nerve cell, every palm-to-palm arrangement a synaptic gap.

When the teacher says 'Go' – the excitatory stimulus to action – the child at the start of the chain touches the palm of the next child lightly with a finger tip, and that child having received the finger-tip message in one hand passes it on with the other hand, and so on right through the one thousand children. The hand that receives the signal is a dendrite. The child's body is the cell. The hand that sends the signal to the next dendritic hand is an axon. Right at the end of the chain the final child would want to make a connection to pass it on. That is what nerves do to muscle fibres or, in the brain, to memory.

The next day the school, having been asked to rearrange itself so that everyone had exactly the same partners as yesterday (though yesterday the partners had been decided by just who happened to be next to each other) would probably see a lot of confusion. But if, day after day, the children adopted the same pattern of association it would gradually become easier and easier and more and more familiar. That is what the brain is busy doing when it learns – though it can send the message through vastly greater numbers of connections in milliseconds. The children might only get a little faster at triggering their palm-to-palm messages, though no doubt they would get faster and better organized than on the first occasion.

Circuits, networks and neural nets

This simple network of children is represented millions of times over for every single piece of information in the brain, all single networks potentially interconnecting with all others. The way the brain organizes all this is only slowly beginning to be understood. The important thing to remember for the moment is that every event is represented by its own network encoded by its own **circuit** and its own neurochemistry. Eighty billion cells each with ten thousand possible connections maybe does not after all sound an oversupply for the job in hand. But the full mystery of how the brain integrates everything it does is still a mystery. And this is the structure within which a coach intends to effect change! No wonder knowing something about it might help.

Knowing about it means, practically, being able to look at the world through your client's eyes – which, in a brain-based model of coaching, is where good coaching starts. It means that the primary task is to understand how your client was grown. What are the primary emotional influences that patterned the person you are setting out to coach? How did your client become the person she is?

Summary

There are two brains at work in a coaching session. One belongs to the coach and one to the client. Both are trying to make sense of the other. Each is sending signals that will materially effect the way the other is working. Both function in the same way but each is quite unlike the other in the detail of the way it was constructed. Both were constructed by and through relationship, and both continue to be hugely influenced by and be the influencer of relationship.

The brain is organized through an extraordinarily complex number of neurochemical connections created by electrical charges between brain cells – 80 billion of them each with the potential for 10,000 connections. Through repeated firing of the same pathways, networks and circuits, patterns are established which encode experience, establish the individuality of each person, and control how people express themselves in all aspects of their lives.

Although the brain is a whole system it is useful to distinguish three major parts – the snake brain, the mammalian brain and the cognitive brain. The way they operate together – and especially the mammalian and the cognitive – is what the modern neurosciences are revealing. The way the mammalian brain and the cognitive brain interlink is key to the practice of coaching based on the science of the brain. Change and development happen essentially through the mammalian brain. All information impinging on the brain – from outside sources as well as inner experience and thoughts – is assessed in the mammalian brain for its emotional significance and distributed into the rest of the brain once that significance has been assessed. The practice of brain-based coaching relies essentially on knowing enough about the brain to use that knowledge to know about the person. The way into knowing about the person is to build a picture of the key influences – and influencers – that shaped the emotional structure of the person you coach. This is the subject of the next chapter.

2 Regulation and relationship
Carrier signals between coach and client

Introduction

The second fundamental proposition running through this book is that:

Your brain is the organ of relationship

by which we mean its capacity to create and respond to all the complex signals that allow us to exist as social beings together. But what are the key elements of 'relationship'? Can we work out what is going on in such a way that a coach and client could understand 'relationship' better and turn it to good use? This chapter examines the emotional origins of the whole of the feeling system, and especially trust and its powerful properties. Then it will be possible to understand the establishment of a relationship that facilitates coaching; why what works, works; and how relationship is the key driver of performance.

Our social nature

Some of the fundamentals of our human existence are of such importance but are so embedded in our experience that we entirely forget to notice them and take them utterly for granted.

In the physical world, water and oxygen both have that characteristic – except, of course, to someone deprived of either of them. They are so necessary for life that if they are in short supply we struggle and if we have none, we die. If we have plenty we tend to use them as givens, on demand. There is also an increasing sense in the Western world that we are so careless of them we waste or pollute them hugely.

Attachment

What if the same were true of key elements of our social existence? What if some aspect of our human experience had the same necessary characteristics to our sustainable social and organizational effectiveness as water and air have to life: that in short supply, we suffer? It is relationship that has this property. Effective human relationship is the means by which the brain develops in the first place and it maintains that power over the brain throughout life. The overarching word for it is *attachment*. The loss of attachment can be so severe that a person can die of a broken heart or shrivel internally through being starved of love. For many people the pain of separation at death or divorce is staggering and entirely unexpected in the way that hurt hits.

> On a late night train leaving Bristol for London, a well-dressed man in his forties sat with tears coursing down his cheeks staring ahead of him. It happened that a skilled counsellor took up a seat opposite him and had settled into her seat before she had seen his distress. After a few minutes, the train having pulled away, she said quietly to him: 'Would you like to talk to someone?' His reply was, 'I've just left my wife and son, and I had no idea how painful it would be. It feels like I've had an amputation without anaesthetic. What have I done to them too? No-one told me it would be like this.'

Attention was first drawn to the survival importance of attachment by some observations in a Chicago orphanage in America in the 1940s. John Bowlby was the first person in the UK who understood their broader significance. Together with Mary Ainsworth (1978) he developed attachment theory – what organizations have now characterized, though at risk of diminishing its significance, as '**engagement**'.

It had been observed in orphanages that infants who were well cared for physically but who were rarely handled beyond the bare necessities failed to thrive. They had a much higher mortality rate than a well-run institution could permit. Bowlby understood that affectionate contact, not just physical care, was a necessity for existence. The lack of it weakened the immune system and increased infant mortality substantially.

Affection

In the 1950s the great American experimental psychologist Harry Harlow used macaque monkeys to systematically explore what attachment was about. In one experiment he had baby monkeys establish relationships with artificial surrogate mothers. There were two kinds of surrogate mothers, though both were a source of food. One surrogate mother was a wire-frame skeleton with a simple head, the other was essentially the same wire-frame skeleton but this time covered with a terry-towelling robe. Baby monkeys infinitely preferred the softer, warmer, terry-towelling 'mother' whatever the level of hunger or availability of food.

A more recent event reflects upon the power of attachment:

> On 27 August 2010 the *Daily Telegraph* newspaper reported a story of how a mother's cuddle brought her new-born baby to life. Two doctors declared the new-born Jamie Ogg dead when he showed no signs of life after being delivered with his twin sister nine weeks premature and weighing only two pounds.
>
> The paper showed a picture of a grieving father and mother cuddling their apparently dead baby between them as they said their farewells. Jamie lay on his mother's chest for two hours. His sister Emily had been rushed off to the neonatal unit. Mother and father spoke to Jamie and kept him close.
>
> Suddenly, after two hours, Jamie began gasping and opened his eyes. Skin-to-skin contact and the human warmth that comes from that had given him life. 'The survival of Jamie . . . has baffled doctors', says the paper. 'Luckily I've got a very strong, smart wife. She instinctively did what she did', said Mr. Ogg.
>
> Doctors are usually baffled when their clinical experience does not fit modern medical knowledge – though almost all medical knowledge becomes redundant remarkably quickly.

Neuroscience is just beginning to make clear how crucial human contact is to well-being. But loving and corporate behaviour do not fit easily together. Or could they? And how is this connected to coaching?

Love

In 1958 Harlow gave a Presidential speech to the American Psychological Association. He called it *The Nature of Love*. 'Thoughtful men and probably all women', he said, 'have speculated on the nature of love'. But he bemoaned the fact that psychologists had generally failed to take any interest in it at all.

> Because of its intimate and personal nature it is regarded by some as an improper topic for experimental research. But our assigned mission as psychologists is to analyze all facets of human and animal behavior into their component variables. So far as love or affection is concerned, psychologists have failed in this mission. . . . Psychologists . . . not only show no interest in the origin and development of love or affection, but they seem unaware of its very existence.

Substitute the word 'manager' or 'executive' or 'HR specialist' or 'OD specialist' or 'executive coach' for 'psychologist'. If you re-run that paragraph by substituting executive coaching for psychologist you will see that the same ideas could apply.

Because of its intimate and personal nature, love is regarded by some as an improper topic for the organizational vocabulary. But our assigned mission as executive coaches is to understand all aspects of executive behaviour and their impact upon performance. So far as love or affection is concerned, executive coaches have been scared of this mission. . . . Management theorists, executive coaches and not least HR specialists . . . not only show no interest in the origin and development of love or affection and its impact on organizational effectiveness, but they seem unaware of its very existence.

Here is how coaches can remedy that state.

Emotions

We have touched briefly on emotions and **feelings**. 'Emotions' are primary and basic feelings whilst 'feelings' are compounds of emotions. And both these words need to be used precisely if executive coaches are going to have a skilled profession based on real science.

Think for a moment of the rainbow. In its amazing spread of colours across the whole spectrum from red to violet, the primary red fades into the orange that has mixed red with the primary yellow; then the green that follows is a mix of yellow with the primary blue; and blue in turn mixes with red to make indigo and violet. The three primary colours in this – red, yellow and blue combine in an infinite variety of ways to make the millions of shades of colour that the rainbow or your computer printer can display. In the same way the primary emotions are the origins of the whole feeling system.

In his ground-breaking book of 1996, *Emotional Intelligence*, Daniel Goleman attempted the first great modern integrated statement about the emotions derived from the neurosciences. Much before that, Darwin had been fascinated by the same subject when in 1872 he published *The Expression of Emotions in Man and Animals*. Nineteenth and twentieth century experimental psychology did not have much space for the emotions, however. The capacity to *think* was seen as the special and dominant capacity of humans, setting them apart from animals and making them the dominant species of the known universe. This is a bias that still exists today and asserts itself in organizations, which like to believe that rational, economic thinking underpins the way that they function. The split between thinking and feeling was fuelled also by Descartes' mind/body dualism and the synthesis of his ideas contained in the aphorism: *I think, therefore I am.*

Darwin's notion about the universality of emotion was supported in the later part of the twentieth century through the work of anthropologist Paul Ekman (1972). Together with Wallace Friesen, Ekman took photographs of people who were displaying a range of emotions and showed them to others around the world, including those in remote tribal areas who had previously had little contact with the rest of the world. He found that they were able to recognize the emotions of those in the photographs; and similarly those in the Western world were able to recognize the facial expressions of these tribal people with a good degree of accuracy. Ekman thus concluded that the recognition and expression of emotions is universal – at least for the basic **emotions**. The face it seems is a rich source of information. Interestingly, not only can facial expressions illuminate the emotional state of another but it also seems that mimicking a facial expression can cause the same physiological effects as the emotion itself – in other words, reproducing a smile can make you feel happier.

Also during the twentieth century, the work of Freud (1938) created an intense awareness of the emotional nature of our psychological existence. His model of a **mind** that contained an *id, ego* and *superego,* driven by unconscious forces, now seems increasingly wrong. It had no foundations in experimental science and consequently it was seen in the hard world of business as 'soft' stuff. But he had an extraordinary effect on turning attention towards the possibility of understanding the dynamics of inner life.

'Neuro-marketing'

That is not to say Freud's ideas were not widely used. The advertising industry was (and is) fascinated by the possibility of being able to predict and play upon 'unconscious forces' in consumers as a way of modifying their behaviour. But the neurosciences are unpicking 'unconscious forces' in terms of the neuro-chemistry of pleasure and addiction. These are the concepts, together with the neuro-economics of risk-taking, that will underpin the advertising industry of the twenty-first century.

Neuroscience is starting to show how people buy for emotional, not economically rational, decisions. Although we typically like to think we behave in a rational way when making decisions, actually that is not what we do though the decisions we take make perfectly good sense to the person making the decision at the time it is made. What the brain does is make sense, within that person's framework, of the decision that the brain has made. In a study that has served to increase the interest of marketers in neuroscience, participants switched preferences between two cola brands once the brands were revealed to them. Brain scans showed that brand A was the preferred product when tasted blind, setting off stronger activity in a brain region associated with the reward system than brand B. However, once the brands were revealed to them, participants reported a preference for brand B. Scans then showed increased activity in the **cerebral cortex** which suggested to researchers that brand knowledge (and the meaning that participants attached to that brand) had overridden the initial taste-based preference (McClure *et al.*, 2004).

Perhaps as we move through the twenty-first century we can now begin to understand that whilst Freud was a great observer he was not a good model builder – despite the almost religious-like practices by which his ideas have been safeguarded and handed down through the practice of psychoanalysis and its many variants in psychotherapy. Freud's methodology was essentially observational not scientific for, as he himself realized, the scientific method for studying the mind that so interested him was simply not available.

Feelings

Science requires a clear and precise language. That is why it is so important to distinguish between emotions and feelings, because with a precise language there is no doubt as to what is meant. With an imprecise language there is lots of room for interpretation. The danger is that interpretation then takes the place of real knowledge and no systematic shared developments in understanding are possible because the knowledge becomes grounded in belief rather than science (as has been the case with much study to do with human behaviour). With a precise language, any personal predilections can be removed from the understanding and a shared common framework found.

The distinction between *emotions* and *feelings* is a particular case of this general proposition, and is helpful in more clearly setting out the case for the brain being the organ of relationship. Emotions are the irreducible feelings. Like the primary colours, they are the elements from which all the other compounds are made. So the primary or basic feelings will be 'emotions'.

Basic emotions

Although there is continuing debate about exactly how many basic emotions there are, the best working answer at the present time is to go on the assumption that there are eight of them.

It is useful, when thinking about the emotions, to remember always that they are the source of motivational energy in the human system. Think e-motions – energy creating movement. It is from the energy contained in an emotion that an individual will get the impetus to take action, which is itself the result of neuro-electrical-chemical circuits being activated in the brain.

Five survival emotions

Five of the eight basic emotions are concerned with escape and avoidance and are the survival emotions. They are what got us here, evolutionarily speaking. They are fear, anger, disgust, shame and sadness, most easily remembered with the mnemonic FADSS. Not only did they get us humans here, they are evident in all other mammals too. They are the drivers that produce flight, fight and freeze and are the most easily triggered of the emotional reactions. The consequences of ignoring a survival emotion are likely to far outweigh the consequences of ignoring any of the other emotions.

1 Potentiator

Then there is one of the emotions that involves **surprise or startle**. We call it a '**potentiator**' as it has the capacity to tip into any one of the other seven emotions. This potentiator, the surprise/startle emotion, creates a lot of energy that is waiting for the potentiated direction to become apparent. There are industries built upon it alone. Think of big-dipper rides or Disney World. What people buy is the opportunity to be surprized and startled followed by the resolution of that state. A big dipper can generate huge amounts of fear and then the relief of being safe. Or think of watching a late-night television show where a stand-up comedian who is developing a joke that, as you watch and listen, you realize might become so disgusting you wish you had the strength of character to switch it off but wonder if it might become side-splittingly funny and an immediate source of joy. Holding an audience at that point and delaying the punch-line increases the intensity of the reaction when it comes if the punch-line is strong enough to carry the weight of the elevated expectation.

2 Attachment emotions

At its best, the punch-line might turn out to belong purely to the attachment emotions – the last two of the eight. They are excitement/joy and love/trust. These two spectra encompass the attachment emotions. They underpin all great human experiences and are the stuff of poetry, drama, art and, fundamentally, enduring relationship and anything at all worthwhile hanging on to in life.

But, strangely, they have *no* survival value. They have enormous human, cultural and social value. They are what most people struggle for, most of their lives. They are what almost all consumer behaviour is based upon. They are what distinguish a great organization from a mediocre one. But they have no primary survival value. That belongs only to the escape/avoidance emotions. But they are what create the best kind of sustainability.

Organizational consequences

The words we use

In the 1960s an American psychiatrist called Eric Berne set out to re-interpret Freud's thinking. He and his colleagues, of whom T. A. Harris is the best known for his book *I'm OK, You're OK* (1967), developed a school of thought and practice called *transactional analysis*, or TA for short. Harris's own initials seem to have been a curious though happy coincidence! Berne set out his thinking in *Games People Play* (1964) and *What Do You Say After You Say Hello?* (1972).

TA took as its starting point the fact that human beings are social animals and that what determines our everyday relationship existence is the words that we use. Within the words are meanings, and TA practitioners are especially fascinated by the meanings underneath the words and how they are both transmitted and received and how those meanings are then the bases of whatever action and reaction follows.

The transactional analysts did not have the benefit of any modern understanding of how the brain works. But they did work out, following Freud, that early emotional patterning created what they called ego states which became the filters by which meaning was assigned to words. These emotionally-based ego states could be seen to come from the experiences of being parented as a child which in turn formed the basic inner directions for social behaviour – what they described as the social transactions between people and which were the focus of their interest and analysis

TA is one excellent example of how acute observers have seen essential truths about how the brain works without having sufficient knowledge upon which to refine their thinking. What is now known is that the eight emotions, transmuted into feelings, underpin all the meaning that we make of the words that we hear, think and say. And we do not have to assume a set of ego states organizing them, useful though the ego states idea was when there was nothing else by which to create an understanding.

Structure of the emotional system

The amygdala

For the moment we have established that there are eight basic emotions. The gateway to the emotional system is entirely guarded, controlled and managed by two almond-shaped systems, one on each of the inner lower surfaces of the temporal lobes (inwards from the ear and a bit forward), called the *amygdala*. They are built into the depths of the brain and linked into all parts of it. Like the most advanced radar system coupled to the finest deep space telescope you can imagine, their function is to assess every single stimulus – piece of information, event, thought, flicker of the imagination, distant sound, smell, slightest touch, glimpse of a person – for its emotional loading. In nanoseconds the amygdala assign that stimulus to its appropriate emotional track. If it is something known, the track is already there. If it is unknown, the track is created out of the emotional system that is part of the hard-wiring with which we come into the world using the database already there.

Think of a busy mainline station like King's Cross, London and the way people pour into the Underground station there at the peak of the evening rush hour. Then think of the linear underground system with all its network connections as being like the brain and the people entering the system as stimuli impinging upon the brain.

In order to get where they want to get to the people going down into the depths of the system have to pass through a ticket barrier. Imagine there are only two. Think of those ticket barriers as the amygdala and the people as signals in the networks of the brain. Passing through the barrier permits a limited number of choices to be made. In the underground system at King's Cross there are five lines to get on to. A choice for any one of them precludes choices for all the rest.

Once on, it is possible to get out at any place that is on that route, and other people (stimuli) will join in but only because that route also has relevance to them. There are occasional junctions where it might be possible to switch to another line, but once the initial choice has been made the options are relatively limited and the longer the person stays on the one line the more the options reduce. Or, put the other way, the more certain the outcomes become.

Assessing stimuli

This is not a bad metaphor for understanding what happens when any signal is being assessed by the amygdala. It gets set on a track (a neural circuit) defined initially by the strongest emotion or feelings associated with it. That is where that stimulus *habitually* wants to go (as the brain is a 'prediction machine' and in recognizing patterns will firstly evoke a habitual response). If it is an entirely new stimulus, the amygdala will make the decision as to where it should go based on a lightning assessment (about eighty nanoseconds) of all relevant prior experience and the nature of the stimulus itself. In this way complex chains and networks of stimuli are built up that then become associated with all sorts of recurring and new events. This is the huge bank of experience from which any one person's brain assumes its own particular characteristics, shape, patterns and identity. So the brain is a highly individualized fluid dynamic store of all our habits, and uses that store to allocate all new experiences to relevant networks.

This huge bank of experience is also a crucial component for the construction of individual identity – the Self.

Unfamiliar stimuli

The way the brain works is well illustrated by what happens when something impinges on the brain for which it has no network storage capacity or familiarity. Listening to Chinese if you have absolutely no familiarity with the language will leave you baffled as to the meaning of what is being said. Your brain has no emotions attached to any recognition of those particular sounds. It could well have had, if chance had found you born in China with Chinese spoken regularly around you. But in the absence of relevant experience, the brain has no basis for action. That's why change is so difficult. It presumes something unknown; and the brain is in any event already busy with what it knows.

Unexpected stimuli

The way the brain works when something traumatic happens is that it is bombarded with confusion of which it has to try to make the best order that it can, for that is its job. In their nature, traumatic events are generally unexpected, the participant in the event is usually an uninvited participant and the immediate event is, by definition, outside their expectation and often right outside their experience.

Such events confuse the brain, as they have no allocated space or network. The brain cannot make sense of such events. There are no reference points. Being the primary sense-making organ, nothing is more affronting to the brain than having something happen that makes no sense – an observation often seen socially when one person, in disbelief at what someone else has just said, says: 'You must be joking!'

Peter

A particular instance of an event that makes no sense might go as follows. Consider a client going to an informal review meeting with their direct boss. Their previous experience of such meetings would have shaped their expectations of how this current conversation might unfold and so now imagine the surprise of this client, Peter, to be 'offered', right out of the blue, redundancy.

This has happened to clients of ours and probably of yours. We understood that Peter's brain struggled to make sense of what had been set out before him. He subsequently described how the emotions he experienced were instantaneous, intense, moving from the surprise/startle potentiator into fear, anger, shame and sadness. Whilst Peter was hearing the words being spoken, he was similarly aware that he was unable to 'take it all in' and his ability to react was severely compromised. His brain was immediately wondering for him how he would survive.

After the meeting, Peter rebuked himself for not having taken notice of the warning signs that redundancy might even be a possibility for him. His employer, whilst doing well at a national level, was undergoing change and reorganization at a local level, as well as having been bought by a larger, overseas company in the preceding year. Nevertheless, Peter had unique and specialist skills that had been valued and rewarded and the reaction of surprise that the 'offer' evoked in his immediate colleagues did much to exacerbate his own confusion.

Coupled with this was fear. Peter had not anticipated losing his job and was anxious about how he would find a new one as well as what being made redundant said about both his abilities and his value to any organization. The supportive comments made by friends, family and colleagues that things might well work out for the better were not experienced as supportive by Peter. Although he understood, on one level, that they might be right, the emotional system in his brain was overwhelming his thinking brain so that he felt out of control: and that experience in itself, being immediately picked up by the amygdala, served only to increase his sense of helplessness. Peter's boss had managed the redundancy process without any special skill or prior thought as to what the emotional consequences for Peter would be. As is so often the case organizationally the imperatives of 'the organization' wreck the human qualities and capacities upon which the best organizations pride themselves and through which they thrive.

The limbic system

The amygdala, whose primary task is to search for whatever might have danger attached to it, were busy directing Peter's imagination into high arousal fear pathways as well as disgust, shame and sadness, and would not easily calm down from such a shock. Behind the amygdala lies the limbic system. It is in the limbic system that the eight emotional highways lie (the tube lines of our King's Cross metaphor). The limbic system mixes the emotions to create *feelings* that are compounds of emotions, just as all colours are compounds of the primary colours, and then distributes the feelings, attached to the stimulus of the event, upwards into the cortex creating neural pathways.

Any experience, any event of any kind, gets feelings (mixes of the emotions) attached to it in the pathways of the brain so that the experience and the feeling combine together to create meaning. This is the basis of meaning which, together with our capacity to encode that into words related to the events, can reconstruct meaning from memory without having to relive the events in actuality. But memory is not like a video that can be played back and always reappears in exactly the same way. Rather it is a storehouse of events attached to feelings which together form experience and which can be modified by both prior and related experiences. Events only have significance to the extent that they have feelings attached to them and feelings from one event can get attached to, or trigger, another. The stronger the feelings the more meaning they will have and hence the more potential for action – unless of course there are strong contradictory feelings, in which case action gets jammed. The more meaning the event has to the person in the context of his or her own life the more likely is that event to have raw emotion attached to it. The most powerful of the raw emotions is fear, for it has the most survival value. From fear all else is overwhelmed. In the absence of fear all possibilities lie open – though the stronger any of the escape/avoidance emotions are the more overwhelming potential they have.

Brain as the organ of relationship

It is through its emotional system that the brain established itself as the primary organ of relationship as well as the primary organ of making sense of what is going on in the world. In some ways they are not such very different capacities. As we have seen, when we are born our survival depends on contact with another human being and, as development proceeds, on our making systematic sense of that contact. The basic emotions that are present in that contact become the basis upon which the developing infant/child/teenager/ young adult makes relationship sense of their world. By absorbing the information that comes to them through the sense-making of the key adults around them transmitted through the emotional, not the intellectual, system, children grow into their own individuality. The intellectual system is for understanding. The emotional system is for experiencing. The whole of the brain is for putting those two elements together, making rational sense of them by integrating them into a whole Self. It is the right-hand half of the brain – the **right hemisphere** – that is mostly focused on the emotional system and new-ness. It is the **left hemisphere** that deals with facts and what is known.

Emotional energy

Primary emotions are the key elements of relationship. And the emotions (remember *e-motion*) are the key source of mobilizing the energy systems of the body in one direction or another. That makes it possible to state, clearly and strongly, that if the escape/avoidance/**survival emotions** (FADSS) are triggered energy will be diverted into self-preservation. Energy will not be available for action other than to the extent it most serves the survival interests of the individual. That is what can create (even long-drawn-out) politicking inside organizations.

If the attachment emotions are triggered, however, then energy flows outwards and, properly directed, into the strategic objectives of the organization as expressed in every tactical undertaking in which the individual engages.

Organizational culture

Walk into a hotel, anywhere in the world, and your first encounter with staff – concierge desk, reception desk, bell boy – will give you a huge amount of immediate information about how that hotel works.

Many years ago, before Hong Kong was handed back to its original owners, the Mandarin Oriental there was a haven of luxury. It may well still be so. At the time from which this story comes the more modern Mandarin stood competing, across the water that separated the island from the mainland via the Star ferry, with the old colonial Peninsula Hotel.

Both were grand and set out to be exemplary in everything they did. At the Peninsula the staff wore tightly-buttoned uniforms and white gloves. The ceilings were high, the decor unremittingly gleaming, and the atmosphere busy. But it was not relaxed. The tightly-buttoned uniforms said it all. There was a sense of staff being on parade and at risk of immediate inspection. Staff manners were wonderful, everyone was courteous, any request was immediately met, and yet. . . . There was no sense of being at ease despite a setting of instant and high level service.

Back at the Mandarin Oriental the ceilings were not so high, though the decor was just as immaculate. Uniforms flowed rather than showed tight buttoning and the slight bows with which requests were met before action was taken were more fluid than at the Peninsula. There was no sense of an imminent inspection and the critical eye that would accompany such an act. What the Mandarin conveyed was sense of welcome, not of being on show. The focus was the visitor's comfort not the staff's presentation.

Trust

Two different pathways within the limbic system are evident in this recollected account of two great hotels at a particular point in their diverse histories. In the Peninsula there was a little sense of fear. Criticism, or the possibility of it, is a great generator of fear or the preparatory defences necessary to thwart it. In the Peninsula it kept staff stiff. Stiffness does not a welcome make however smartly it is done.

In the Mandarin there was no obvious sign of the possibility of fear. In their entire manner, style and dress Mandarin staff created a sense of warmth without the expectation of being inspected at any moment. Doubtless there were from time to time highly critical guests who found cause, warranted or otherwise, for loud complaint. But that was not the expectation that the staff had. They conveyed the opposite – that the guest's experience would be one of real pleasure of which they were the accomplished facilitators. There was a level of self-regulated confidence in the Mandarin staff that was missing in the Peninsula's.

Such a difference comes from management, of course. If management has done a superb job it is embedded within the culture of the organization and gets passed to new staff as they join in and become a real part of a team in the continuous creating of a style and a tradition. The most senior management creates the organizational culture.

But from where within management does it come?

The answer is: the limbic system. And the special bits of the limbic system that are in play both on the receiving (staff) and transmitting (management) side are the amygdala. In this particular example what the Mandarin management culture had embodied within its staff was that management trusted staff and, in consequence, the staff trusted themselves. The emotion that the amygdala were conveying was *trust*.

That then is what the amygdala of the staff conveyed to the amygdala of an arriving guest: trust in themselves and their capacity to deliver, simultaneously in all the systems that backed them up, and also simultaneously in their colleagues to act in a coherent manner based upon that trust. The trust came from, and also engendered, a sense of how to *be*. At the Peninsula the emphasis was on how to *perform*. That is not a generator of trust.

The Inner Game of Tennis (1975), described by W. Timothy Gallwey, shares some of the principles that have just been described and his approach is familiar to many coaches.

Emerging in the first instance from a sporting context, Gallwey (1975: 11) suggests that 'every game is composed of two parts, an outer game and an inner game . . . neither mastery nor satisfaction can be found . . . without giving some attention to the relatively neglected skills of the inner game'.

In each of us, he goes on, there are two selves, evident in the conversations that we have in our own minds. Self 1 he characterizes as the 'teller' that issues instructions and commands, judges performance and chastises, whilst Self 2 is the 'doer' and includes the non-conscious mind and the nervous system. Self 1 cannot bring itself to trust Self 2 'even though the unconscious, automatic self is extremely competent' and from this might emerge a cycle of events which sees Self 1 get in the way of Self 2 performing to the best of its ability.

In simple terms, Self 1 can create a set of 'interferences' which might in themselves become the focus of attention in any efforts to improve performance but which actually, if they were taken out of the equation, would free up Self 2 to show up without limitation.

In his book, *The Inner Game of Work* (2002), Gallwey describes how he applied these principles to a piece of work he undertook in a corporate call centre environment. The task set was to increase courtesy scores, but rather than attack this head on by imposing a list of actions or behaviours to induce more courtesy, for instance, he began from the premise that if their Self 1 interference was quietened then Self 2's 'courtesy would be expressed as a natural consequence'.

It emerged that operators were dealing with boring, repetitive jobs that were stressful because of the level of monitoring and measurement. As a consequence a programme was designed to reduce stress and boredom (Self 1 interferences) and to increase enjoyment, eliciting from participants their experience of what might help to do that. Ultimately operators recognized that 'quite a lot could be learned if you listened' – qualities in the voice such as warmth, stress, friendliness, which could then be matched by them expressing different qualities in their own voices which in turn led to improved courtesy scores.

Although this is apparently an organizational/management story, it is a surprisingly accurate metaphor of the coach's relationship with a client.

Essential ingredient to coaching

A client finds themselves in an encounter with a coach, and vice versa, neither of them knowing much of the other. It is the same with a first visit to an unknown hotel. In both cases there might have been prior recommendations and information available, but the actual encounter is the decider as to what follows. The coach may adopt the Pensinsula solution. However urbane the coach might be, somewhere in the back of her head is some circulating anxiety about whether she will get the assignment, whether she will be good enough and meet the client's expectations, what the outcome will be. There is a self-critical note apparent in the meeting and the encounter is established with unwritten – even, maybe, written – performance criteria in mind. The coach may do a good job in whatever sessions are subsequently available, and the client may report himself as highly satisfied. But as both came from a critical, perform-ance-led culture no other expectations were in the room. Cultural and performance expectations were met to a Peninsula standard, which is pretty high.

On the other hand the coach could adopt the Mandarin solution and profoundly trust her own background capabilities as a coach, know she does not know everything and be equally aware that she knows when she does not know and what is to be done when such a situation arises (like use the client to find out). Then client and coach can approach the coaching encounter not with a background of performance anxiety but in the spirit of shared enquiry and discovery. Such an approach generates trust.

Then something extraordinary happens. As trust starts to flow between coach and client the client's limbic system starts opening up to new options and possibilities *because* the primary danger-seeking function of the amygdala quietens down. It is at this point that the coach can start to do what a good coach does best – begin to facilitate the client's brain in an exploration of the possibilities that have hitherto been unexplored.

Summary

The brain is the organ that is created by, manages and is managed by relationship. 'Relationship' can be between two (or more) people or the relationship of the individual with themself. For the brain, the key information in relationship comes from the eight basic emotions attached to words and actions. Trust is the most fundamental of the attachment emotions. It creates energy unhampered by the destructive side of stress or performance anxiety. Such energy can flow outwards into achieving whatever goals might be wanted.

3   Oxytocin and other clever chemicals

Introduction

Third fundamental proposition for the whole book:

> *The brain is an extraordinary neuro-chemical factory and the brain-based coach needs to know enough about that to use it in coaching.*

Making connections

The brain is more wet-ware than hardware. The eighty billion cells of the brain are like the three trillion cells of the rest of the body except that they have acquired the specialized function of transmitting electro-chemical messages. When a stimulus of sufficient strength creates an action potential within one or more of the 80 billion cells (neurons) that the brain contains, this action potential is evidenced by a nerve cell generating an electrical current.

Axons

Extending from that nerve cell is a fibre called an 'axon'. The axon can be as long as the width of a human hair or anywhere up to two metres long. The action potential travels down the axon as an electrical current triggering the release of chemical molecules when it gets to the tip of the fibre.

There are several thousand miles of these nerve cells and their axons in the brain. Each of the 80 billion neurons has the possibility of connecting to 10,000 other cells. Try 80 billion × 10,000 to get some sense of the extraordinary complexity of the brain's networks.

Dendrites

Information, in the way of chemical changes, is passed into cells through receiving fibres called dendrites. So axons pass information to dendrites.

Whilst there is only one axon to each cell (though the axon may have many branches at its tip), there are many dendrites receiving information from axons and passing that information via electrical stimulation into the body of the receiving cell for onward transmission.

Synapses

The cells and their axons transmit to the dendrites of other cells not by being physically connected but by creating chemical discharges at the tips of each **axonal fibre** for passing across a gap, known as a synapse or synaptic gap, and offering the discharge of chemical molecules to the receiving dendrites of the next cell down the track. Thus the circuits of the brain are built up by the frequency or intensity with which any particular pathway is excited. This is the basis of associative learning – the way the brain builds and somehow stores its fluid banks of memory experience. The cells that fire together wire together – though it is beginning to be seen as more a hiring than a wiring process.

We have used the 'pile of bricks' metaphor and the image of schoolchildren in the playground as a way of trying to give some sense of how the basic building blocks of brain cells can be put together in almost any form; but once put together will tend to exist more readily in that pattern than any other.

Glial cells

For the sake of completeness it is also important to know that there is a second kind of cell in the brain. The neurons are the messenger system of the brain. There are also millions of cells called **glial cells**. These cells have two main functions. The first is to act as the housekeepers for the neurons – tidying up waste and keeping the system healthy. The second is to create **myelin**.

Myelin is a fatty substance created by the glial cells and wrapped around circuits that are most frequently used. Myelination both protects the circuit and especially the cell body itself and increases the speed of transmission within that circuit. When we refer to 'brain cells' in any form we are talking about the messenger cells, the neurons, rather than the housekeeper glial cells.

Nerve impulses in the brain flow in only one direction. In the receiving, dendritic fibres there will be receptors waiting to receive the neurotransmitter chemical molecules from the axon that has been stimulated to release its chemicals into the synaptic gap. Depending on what else is happening at the gap, as well as the strength of the signal, and the existence of exactly the right receptors for the chemicals that are being discharged, the signal that has been triggered will or will not pass into the next cell, and so on down the chain of any particular circuit. This can be modified by such things as tiredness, anger, excitement, too much alcohol the night before, worrying about the difficult client in the day ahead, and so on.

Neurochemicals

Each neurochemical has a different shaped molecule that is particular to that neurochemical alone. Molecular transmission and take-up across the synaptic junctions depends upon there being exactly the right-shaped receptor in the dendrite(s) for receiving the molecule(s) being transmitted, and also that nothing else is interfering with the transmission. It is like one of those early learning toys where a child learns to post different shapes through a lid into a box. Only a triangle will get into the box through a triangular-shaped posting hole, a star shape through a star-shaped hole, a square through a square hole, and so on. It is exactly the same with **neurochemicals** from the axon getting into the receptors of the dendrite.

If the box into which the shapes were to be posted had treacle smeared across it, or someone had stuck Sellotape across some of the posting holes, the shapes would not fit, or would get stuck in the attempt to make them fit in.

That is exactly what happens at the synaptic gap when something is happening within the neurochemistry of the brain to interfere with the straightforward uptake of the molecules from axon to dendrite. Your clients' inner rage at the way they are being treated at work will create a chemical discharge across synaptic gaps – **cortisol**, for instance – that will prevent, say, normal creative processes flowing, or loving a spouse appropriately, or finding time and energy to praise a member of staff for something well done.

Coaching

What as a coach would you do with the following situation?

Jim

A busy executive who spent more time getting on and off aeroplanes than he cared to think about, Jim arrived back at his home town one Friday evening after a fortnight away and yet another exhausting round of meetings on two widely separated continents. The creative director for an international branding company, his job was to stimulate and maintain other people's creativity around the world, and he was reckoned to be good at doing that.

Sally, Jim's wife, was at the airport to meet him. She was keen to talk on the hour's car journey home about what had been happening domestically for the past fortnight, the children's various triumphs at school, and especially what had been happening in the extensive redesign and building works she was overseeing at their home. She understood he was tired, noticed he was hardly responding, but thought she could ease him into his return by talking about the things she thought were of joint interest to them. But something she said about a bit of the mechanics of the gym-room redesign she had had to get on with in his absence triggered a hugely aggressive response in Jim. He swore at her in the most offensively sexual way possible. That did not make for the beginnings of the weekend Sally had been hoping for, weary as she herself was with carrying all the family responsibilities in Jim's ever-frequent absences and now with her hopes for the weekend dashed. She went completely cold and quiet. And Jim sat cursing under his breath to himself. That is how they got home, and barely spoke all weekend. Sally had a busy programme arranged for the children. Jim only wanted to watch an international soccer game throughout Saturday afternoon and slept late on Sunday.

Jim had a coaching session planned for the following Tuesday. His coaching contract had been set up because his CEO had heard around the company that, brilliant though Jim was, there were occasions when he would take another person apart emotionally during one-on-one sessions and always for reasons that seemed trivial to the other person. Jim had agreed with his CEO that he could sometimes lose his rag, but it was always with the best intentions for the output reputation of the company. But the CEO was becoming troubled by the damage both to individuals and the company that Jim might be causing and on that basis an initial six-month coaching contract had been set up.

The 'real me'

When a person loses control in the way that Jim was known to do in the company, and in his homecoming with Sally, to the great but bottled-up misery of them both, he is being just the same person at work and at home *as we all are*. There is a myth popular in high-striving organizations that people can adopt some kind of persona when they come to the office, leaving the 'real me' at home.

That is simply not possible. The persona in the office is as much part of the 'real me' as the person who is allegedly left at home. What is typically happening in the office is that a set of rules have been agreed, usually explicitly but implicitly too as part of the culture in well-established organizations, about how you will behave at work. That 'me' has agreed with the rules and may well unknowingly use up a lot of energy keeping them in place. But without a 'real me' having agreed to keeping the rules they would not be kept in any way at all. It's the 'real me' that organizes the 'work me'. It's quite a waste of energy.

Of course the agreement with company rules may not be heartfelt. One person may have agreed because the sanctions for not agreeing are severe; another because it is the line of least resistance; yet another because 'that is the game round here'. Nevertheless, it is a 'real me' that is managing these internal balancing acts. The dilemma arises when there are competing 'me's operating within the whole 'me'. The Jim who likes to be liked and creates a great deal of enthusiasm sometimes operates in one-to-ones as a real destroyer or swears viciously at the wife he says he loves.

The evidence from the neurosciences makes it clear that it is early neural patterning formed in the experiences of key relationships that constructs the patterns of later adult life behaviour. From within its huge potential the brain learns about its own particular world in the context of the experiences that give colour to life and fix the pathways of the brain. That is what the emotions do. As the patterning becomes familiar so the brain tends to see the world in terms of what it already knows. The brain doesn't start life with a template of how things should be. It simply learns how things are. That is what shapes our own reality.

Here is what happened next with Jim

Jim arrived at the coaching session, his fourth, planned for a couple of hours, clearly on edge and unsettled. The coach asked him immediately what was worrying him, and Jim moved straight into an account of his wife's coldness all weekend, how stressful he had found that, and how after such a weekend he really couldn't get any energy flowing in himself or other people in the office the previous day, which is what he said was really worrying him and wanted to talk about.

What would you do with such a situation?

The responses we have actually had from coaches when discussing this material vary from: 'I would have suggested he got his wife to go and see a marriage counsellor', to: 'I can't imagine a coaching session where someone like Jim would come to talk with me like that', to: 'Coaching is really about performance, isn't it, not about relationships?'

Coaching the whole person

Our view is that any client brings to any coaching session the only thing that she or he can bring, which is him- or her-*Self*. The whole of the person is always present in the room. And it is the coach's special professional responsibility both to know that and respond to the whole of the Self. Because it is *from* the Self that all behaviour comes; and it is only *in* the Self that effective change happens.

When we say that, many coaches say: 'But that's really therapy you're talking about. That's not my job as a coach. Therapy is about sorting out the past. As a coach I'm interested in the future.'

To which we reply: 'What you have in front of you in a coaching session is, simply, the whole person. Your client can be nothing more than his or her own past. In knowing the past you can begin to model the future. Without the past you can create with your client an *idea* of how the future might be, you can even create hope for the future. But that is not real systemic change in the client, which is what we imagine you are interested in and what we believe coaching is all about. For if the future person is to be in some ways a *different* person, your client can only become that because your coaching creates actual change in the pathways in the brain. The person in the present *is* their past. And if you do not know about the past and understand as much as you can about the whole person then you won't know what it is you are trying to change. And so if you do not know where "here" is it is pretty unlikely you will get "there".'

Neurochemistry

Here is some understanding of what might be happening in your client's neurochemistry that will give you the beginnings of some way into such a situation as Jim's:

The speed at which the synaptic/dendritic transmission mechanism works is extraordinary. A nerve impulse can travel up to two hundred miles an hour. In the space of a brain that is instantaneously. Your brain can receive and respond to complex signals within 80 milliseconds, which is well before your consciousness can make any sense of what is happening. That takes at least a quarter of a second.

This is taking place among the hundred known chemical agents operating within the brain – and there may be more. The potential cocktail mix at any one synaptic gap is vastly variable. That is what accounts for the exquisitely nuanced shades of difference you can have in both meaning and sensation. Nothing of any kind happens to you without there being an electro-chemical basis for what is happening. Each exquisiteness you experience will have its own chemical mix and its own special circuitry. That is what, together, creates your inner awareness of complexity. Your, or your client's, capacity to put words to that, however, will depend upon the way you have been taught to define and refine inner experience. Complexity is a property of the brain. Actually *recognising* that complexity comes from articulated experience.

Excitation and inhibition

There is one other thing about the chemical messenger system that is important. A chemical instruction can either send a message forward or block it. In this way the brain acts in a binary circuit fashion, with 'gates' (the axonal, synaptic gap, dendritic sequence) saying 'pass' or 'do not pass'. In such a way particular pathways are excited (put into action) or **inhibited** (prevented from taking action). From this 'pass/do not pass' process every circuit is defined.

Uptake process

When the right number of molecules have got their chemical message across, to send the signal onwards or block it, they pass back across the synaptic gap to be taken up again by the transmitting axon. This **re-uptake** process is crucial in the effectiveness of the way messages are transmitted. It is only through having a supply of the right chemicals at the axonal point that another message coming from the cell down the axonal fibre can be transmitted again.

The main neurochemicals

So what are these chemicals by which your behaviour, thoughts, feelings and your Self are all controlled? We are not going to list the whole hundred. For everyday coaching purposes we are going to describe the main chemicals and the key effects that they have.

The main neurochemicals of which you need to know something are to do with attachment, motivation, feeling good, pleasure, and pain relief. These are all created by molecular processes waiting to be released at the ends of axons and collected by the receiving dendrites. There are also various glands in the body that release other chemicals, **hormones**, directly into the bloodstream. They form the **endocrine system** and they have a huge effect upon behaviour. There are seven main **glandular systems**. For coaching purposes two are of particular concern. These two endocrine glands are the **pituitary** and **adrenal**. The **adrenal gland** is especially concerned with that ever-present issue in coaching, stress.

It is the neurochemicals (often referred to a 'neurotransmitters' because they are involved in the transmission of nerve impulses in the brain) and hormones whose effects we are going to describe now.

Attachment

Attachment, the deeper condition of what organizations like to call 'engagement' but generally do not know how to manage systemically – is fuelled by **oxytocin**. Oxytocin evokes feelings of contentment, reduces anxiety and fear, and creates feelings of calmness and security especially around people who are trusted or loved. It is a crucial chemical for establishing effective mother–infant relationships and may be much more profoundly important in organizations than is commonly understood. As the neurochemical basis of trust it is perhaps the basis of moral behaviour.

Motivation

Motivation is a huge word, but at its heart lies something to do with gearing up directional energy appropriately. The *direction* that energy takes is to do with emotions – the processes that create meaning for any one individual. But the energy itself is to do with arousal, and arousal is closely linked to **dopamine** levels. Dopamine controls arousal in many parts of the brain and is vital for giving physical motivation. Levels that are too high give rise to hallucinations, when an over-energized brain is operating and can't distinguish objective from subjective reality. Low dopamine levels reduce sex drive, lower attention, impair sleep and create night sweats.

Feeling good

Feeling good is the special purpose of **serotonin**. It has a particular effect on the management of mood and anxiety. High levels of it correlate with feelings of serenity and optimism. It is also involved in managing sleep, pain, appetite and blood pressure.

Pleasure

Pleasure is the special prerogative of **noradrenaline**. It functions as an enhancer of mood, and may work across all mood states to make them more intense.

Pain relief

Pain relief comes from natural-occurring opiates in the brain called **endorphins** (as well as **enkephalins** and **dynorphins**). Morphine and **codeine** are similar. Endorphins modulate pain, reduce stress and promote a sensation of calm, detached well-being. They also depress physical functions like breathing and may produce physical dependence.

If you have a physical accident, endorphins spontaneously rush in to kill the pain. Interestingly they do not appear in response to emotional pain. So while you can remember, sometime after an accident, that you suffered physical pain, it is not possible to recreate the intense sensation of that pain. With emotional events that have caused pain, and which studies have shown trigger much the same circuits in the brain as does physical pain, the memory of the event *can* re-activate the sensation. So it is probable that the endorphins have a specific effect upon memory circuits too. Another time that endorphins come into play is when people fall in love. They create a natural high. Coupled with serotonin, oxytocin and noradrenaline pumping round the system at the same time it is not surprising that falling in love can lead to remarkably disruptive decisions and be a powerful controller of what to others might seem like completely irrational behaviour even though to the person in love it seems compellingly clear-sighted.

Hormones

The two main hormone-producing glands that concern coaching are the pituitary and the adrenals.

The pituitary gland is located deep within the middle part of the base of the brain and is about the size of a pea. The pituitary gland secretes nine hormones that are to do with maintaining steady state functioning in the body. Its most important function, from a coaching point of view, is that it produces both oxytocin (attachment) and endorphins (pain suppressants). So it is a key element in creating the working relationship upon which good coaching relies.

The adrenal glands sit just above the kidneys, and are responsible for releasing hormones in response to stress, particularly the hormone cortisol.

Stress

The body is extremely well-designed to deal with stress. Without appropriate pressures (stresses) human beings seem to lapse into a kind of torpor. They need stimulating to be at their most effective. Indeed, all effective human societies have created conditions where actively seeking out the challenges that come from self- or socially-imposed pressure is variously rewarded. The whole of the nervous system is designed to deal well with stress.

But this is true only for the short term. The design was established at a time of evolutionary history when physical rather than psychological stress was the predominating condition. Those two facts – short term and physical stress – are no longer the main operating conditions for vast numbers of people in the developed working worlds of the twenty-first century.

Arguably, executive coaching is one of the key adaptive responses to the intolerably chronic stresses under which many executives find themselves labouring. Work stresses are more usually psychological than physical, though they often manifest themselves in physical ways. There has, for instance, in the Western world, over the past twenty years, been a completely unexpected increase in the incidence of heart attacks in otherwise healthy men in their forties and early fifties. The cause of this is being put down to the persistently stressful psychological conditions of long hours, continuous anxiety, impossible objectives and unrealistic performance demands that is the daily lot of many who inhabit modern organizations. The body communicates in its own terms by calling a halt to what is happening. Depression is another similar response of the body saying; 'Slow down round here and look at what is happening to you'.

Cortisol is the effective agent in a lot of this. It is often described as the corrosive chemical, as under some conditions it can actually kill off neurons. The essential purposes of cortisol are to increase blood sugar through helping to keep blood glucose levels within critical limits; to suppress the immune system; and to aid in fat, protein and carbohydrate metabolism. Small increases of cortisol have some positive effects. They produce –

- A quick burst of energy for survival reasons
- Heightened memory functions
- A burst of increased immunity
- Lower sensitivity to pain
- Help in maintaining the balance of all functions of the body

But prolonged and unnecessarily high levels of cortisol in the bloodstream have been shown to be associated with adverse effects such as:

- Impaired cognitive performance
- Suppressed thyroid function
- Blood-sugar imbalance such as hyperglycaemia
- Decreased bone density
- Decrease in muscle tissue
- Raised blood pressure
- Lowered immunity and impaired inflammatory responses such as slower wound healing
- Increased abdominal fat
- Higher levels of 'bad' cholesterol

Hypothalamic-pituitary-adrenal (HPA) axis

The pituitary and adrenal glands are linked in a special circuit by a part of the brain that is called the hypothalamus. The circuit is called the **hypothalamic-pituitary-adrenal axis (HPA**, sometimes HTPA). The hypothalamus is a sort of master controller of many parts of the working nervous system. It links the nervous system and the endocrine system of the glands together

Under ordinary conditions of stress, the hypothalamus sends a message to the front part of the pituitary asking it to tell the adrenal glands to release cortisol to deal with stress. What swings into gear are the good effects of cortisol that we described earlier. The system tunes up – a bit like putting a foot on the accelerator of a car in such away that you create a smooth surge of power to deal with whatever the external conditions are.

But under conditions of continuing stress the HPA circuit becomes over-stimulated – like managing the accelerator badly and flooding the engine. The engine becomes lumpy and at worst may stall. With the HPA axis the hypothalamus keeps responding to the stress demands, keeps instructing the pituitary to make the adrenals work, and thereby creates the continuous loop of sending cortisol into the system which begins to have negative effects, especially on lowering cognitive performance, creating poor sleep and setting up a pattern of ruminative, early-morning waking. The symptoms of stress then become the cause of stress.

At work the person typically begins to feel they have lost their edge, worries about it, finds they are going through the motions though beginning to feel low in energy, adopts the usual solution of ignoring what is happening and trying harder, and thereby creates even more chronically stressed conditions. Over long periods of time the immune system suffers, hair thins, and a deep sense of tiredness sets in. These are the conditions under which a person takes a break and becomes ill immediately.

Neurochemistry and coaching

So how is all this chemistry relevant to coaching? In Jim's case you can see that he intermittently loses his adaptive edge completely. Then he blames other people for the conditions that he himself creates or justifies his actions on the basis of meeting what he considers to be the company's requirements. One way and another he is seriously lacking in insight into his own behaviour and its effects upon others, and is putting the key relationships of his adult life – both his company and his marriage – at risk.

As a means of confronting him with the crucial need to change, a brain-based coach can begin to show Jim how his brain is working. The coach has a chance to make sense for Jim of himself, about himself and to show him what is happening to him, from hard knowledge, not just descriptive supposition. It seems that in executives, who are restless for good information on which to base decisions, understanding that the brain is acting within its own rules even if the behaviour seems to others to be irrational starts the process of re-appraisal and change happening. Perspectives shift, judgements start changing and new perceptions start creating less rigidity in the system.

Equally importantly though, the brain-based coach might also work from understanding that if the brain only knows what it knows, somewhere along life's track Jim has learnt to get his own way by the strategy he is still using. At some stage it must have been a real winning gambit. The fact that it now has the seeds of destruction built into it, at a different time of his life and in different circumstances to when it was set up, is not something that Jim's brain could, of itself, have seen.

So Jim is at risk of being taken by his own mechanisms into some unpleasant outcomes – a legal action of some kind at work and an unhappy marriage or the prospect of divorce. The brain-based coach has some verifiable knowledge about his situation from which to start the process of change.

The essential proposition of brain-to-brain based coaching is that nothing happens in a coaching session without the brain's chemistry being the controller of what is happening. 'The brain's chemistry' is operating in both the coach and the client. It is the coach's job to create the conditions which facilitate the change in the client's brain functions required by the coaching contract. And it is our contention that knowing what the chemicals are that you are trying to affect in both yourself and your client will have a beneficial effect upon that outcome. This can only increase your professionalism, and also aid the development of the profession of coaching as a whole. In Chapters 5, 6 and 10 we will develop those thoughts in practice.

Summary

The brain is more wetware than hardware. A complex neurochemical environment creates the conditions under which information is transmitted by electrical impulses triggering chemical interaction between individual brain cells. Neurochemicals combined with hormones are responsible for the specifics of all human behaviour. All psychology is, in essence, neurobiology, though science is only at the beginning of unravelling the mysteries of that understanding. Understanding the basic neurochemistry of the brain gives a coach both insights into what is happening to a client and a means of explaining to a client why what is being experienced is being experienced.

4 Wondering
The basis for knowing and change

Models, models, models

Anyone now old enough to be an executive coach grew up in a twentieth century that generated a remarkable number of 'models' for, allegedly, explaining and often modifying human behaviour. From the id, ego and superego of Freudian psychoanalysis to the collective unconscious of Jung, to the individualism of Adler and Rollo May and Victor Frankl's variations of humanistic existentialism: from Maslow's developmental motivational ideas, and Albert Ellis's Rational Emotional Behaviourism, many ideas came. This is a list that would also need to include classical Pavlovian and operant Skinnerian conditioning, the whole of applied learning theory, the more seductive models of Leary's transhumanism and eight-circle model of consciousness, the development of Gestalt ideas, Transactional Analysis, neurolinguistic programming and cognitive behaviour therapy in its various forms. There can hardly have been a decade of the twentieth century in which there were not at least two new models being proposed.

So the twentieth century was not short on *models* of human behaviour. What it lacked was *facts*. In the absence of facts the vacuum got filled by theories being asserted as if they were facts. And training to use these assertions developed more as a matter of personal attachment to an idea and 'belonging' to one school of thought or another than the pursuit of a common body of knowledge founded on a science that had, at its heart, a common set of assumptions. That is not a great track record for a hundred years of endeavour in an age of modern communications.

The twentieth century also shifted from the nineteenth century's fascination with understanding the material world into a great surge of interest in what inner worlds were about. At the beginning of the twentieth century the earliest form of X-ray photographs appeared and for the first time medicine could begin to see *inside* the working or damaged body. That was much better than only having post-mortem information. At the end of the same century the capacity to see inside the working brain, through **fMRI** scans and related techniques, developed exponentially. That is also much better than post mortem.

It is the case that a great deal of the applied psychology of the twentieth century came from the demands of the clinical field – as much of the neurosciences still does. Maslow is perhaps the major exception to this in pursuing an understanding of people by studying the top one per cent of effective college students. In doing so he expressed himself somewhat robustly for modern sensibilities in his main 1954 work *Motivation and Personality* when he averred that he was deliberately avoiding the 'study of crippled, stunted, immature and unhealthy specimens (that) can yield only a cripple psychology and a cripple philosophy'. But the point he was making had some substance in it, and his hierarchy of needs is often the only piece of organizational psychology that an executive knows.

What twentieth-century psychology did well was spawn schools of counselling and psychotherapy. It is said in clinical circles that there are more than four hundred different kinds of psychotherapy and counselling. The Good Therapy organization lists one-hundred-and-thirty-seven different *types* of psychotherapy, many having subcategories of practice. The United Kingdom Council for Psychotherapy gets it down to thirty types whilst The Royal College of Psychiatrists lists six. Whatever classification you choose, there is a great deal of it about even if not much agreement as to what 'it' actually is. No wonder that executive coaches do not wish to enter such a polyglot professional system and want, instead, to distinguish themselves from anything to do with the therapy field.

But the majority of coaching training nevertheless draws, one way or another, on clinical models. It is all that has been available. Trying to shift out of the clinical field into, for instance, theories of motivation does not help much. The same model-building and theorizing that lacks an underlying agreed conceptual structure against which ideas can be systematically tested is evident there too. In *Motivating Humans: Goals, Emotions and Personal Agency Beliefs* (1992), Ford recorded thirty-one theories of motivation and added a thirty-second in a brave attempt to integrate them all. That sounds much like the psychotherapies.

Neuroscience for coaches

What the neurosciences have to offer to executive coaches is a way out of the applied psychological morass of the twentieth century and into becoming the leaders of applied neuroscience for the understanding and development of human beings within the corporate world. That might be a cause for real wonder.

Wonder

Would that itself – that **wonder** – create change? It might. At least it would be an interesting test of the model. This is how it would work.

One of the eight basic emotions is 'surprise/startle', which is the basis of 'wonder'. Start from there. Then recall what the eight basic emotions are and try the idea of them as a colour palette, making subtle feeling combinations possible. 'Wonder' has in it the beginnings of attachment – a little (preparatory) excitement, perhaps, and some potential for joy.

What is happening in the brain in this process?

The experience that you will be having at this moment will seem to be entirely to do with thought. But with a little reflection and remembering about neurochemistry you will find that the thoughts themselves are loaded with feelings of greater or lesser intensity. The amygdala are instantly picking up all the subtlety of those feelings and in the same instant testing them against your bank of experience, and creating energy for action as a result – or not, as the case may be.

Simon

Simon hated biology at school, got out of anything to do with science and maths as soon as he could and was much more fascinated by the literary and visual arts, history and languages. Here he is, pretty successful as an executive coach, after a good career in marketing, being asked to start thinking about (for him) difficult things like neuroscience *from which he had detached a long time ago*.

Simon has heard about this neuroscience stuff, vaguely, and that has been enough to attract him to the title he is reading. He might be able to say, rationally, within himself: 'This book makes some sense, I can see what the authors are suggesting and what the future of coaching might be about from their point of view. But does it generate real energized curiosity for me? Honestly? No, not really. Am I going to put time and effort into learning a lot about this? No, probably not. Will I take a chance on the coaching skills that I have continuing to serve me in the future as they have in the past? Yes, probably. Does a bit of doubt remain about that decision? Yes, a bit, but I can live with it.'

From feelings to behaviour

In the whole of that you can begin to sense, by making this process conscious, what the feeling system is up to. It is exactly the same when you are shopping for a new pair of shoes or a suit, or choosing what to take off the supermarket shelves. Feelings that come from mixes of the eight basic emotions entirely manage the behavioural outcomes of every single situation in which you find yourself second by second of every day – and of more of the night than you can recall.

For Simon, 'wondering' *in this context* (for these matters are always contextual), is attached to feelings of dislike that he has not had to bother about since he escaped them by going into the arts sixth form at school. But they are still there. And in context they influence his decisions and actions. It would require a shift in his feelings for his actions to be different. He prefers to stay essentially the same, though the doubt that he felt at the end may stay as a motivator to reconsider his choices at some later stage.

Andrew

Andrew is a senior manager on the sales side of the oil industry. After twenty successful years with the same company it has been suggested to him, in an annual review that, to facilitate his progress to higher general management levels within the company, he should spend the next two years in HR. That is not what he had been expecting out of the review.

Andrew is one of two hundred people worldwide who have been selected as the future general management talent pool for the company. A lot of resources are being pumped into the talent pool and his coaching sessions are a part of that process

Andrew was surprised to have been selected into the pool. He had seen himself as reasonably successful in his career to date but as not especially ambitious. Just over two years ago he had declined, without much anguish or any regrets, a career-accelerating posting to Africa. He had declined, ostensibly, because of his wife's unwillingness to go there because of her job in educational television and his children's schooling. Truth to tell, the prospect of Africa had not interested Andrew himself. It made the working spouse and educational choice 'reasons' for not taking up the offer easy to promote.

In being surprised at having been selected into the future talent pool, Andrew had had a continuing sense that the choice was slightly misplaced – as if he were there under false pretences. But it had given him some stirring of more ambition than previously, not least because he had begun to imagine a financial future that was more substantial than he had been expecting. Being in the pool was not something that he had discussed much with his wife who, with some green credentials of her own, privately thought the oil industry was not the right thing to be in though she was not averse to its income benefits.

So here you are in a coaching session with Andrew who has told you of his doubts about the HR suggestion. In discussion you find that the idea he should spend a couple of years in HR has come from a newly-appointed HR talent development manager who Andrew has met but did not especially like. You yourself know that spending time in HR was not in the original big plan outline for members of the talent pool and that, as far as Andrew knows, no-one else is being offered the same development track.

Where, as a brain-based coach, would you go with this? Andrew is looking for support in making 'the right decision'. How often have you heard that? What

will get Andrew to the right decision? Do you deal with the situational prag-
matics of the decision – his dislike of the development manager, his insecurities
about being part of the talent pool, his apparently reactive personality? Your brief
in the coaching programme is a general one of having twelve sessions over two
years to support Andrew in his development and here you are in session three.

Where you go depends on your capacity to be in Andrew's head and
sort out the muddle and uncertainties as if you were him but functioning with
greater clarity. And simultaneously, from that perspective, to work out
and implement how he can make the choice for himself. It is what a good
parent does with a child, and what the neural mechanisms of attachment are
for in the working design of the brain. You, the coach, are to act as the emotional
regulator of Andrew's internal world. As you do this he will begin to find his
own way to regulate his own system. Then he will have the capacity to make a
decision that is his and, more importantly, *feel* that it is his. That is what brain-
based coaching is about. That way you will discover what the emotional load-
ings are within the options that Andrew has and that will precipitate his
decision.

A simple way of reflecting on this task is to think of a child with a small
amount of money in a shop trying to decide, in the face of seriously competing
possibilities, what to spend that money on. The indecision is palpable. A wise
parent doesn't simply tell the child what to buy – though unwisely many
a parent, in a rush to move on or 'not waste money', might well do so. A wise
parent creates the conditions under which the child makes the decision
and makes the outcomes her own. The parent has understood the child's
indecision – has been able to look at the world through the child's eyes – and
then has created the conditions under which, bit by bit, that child becomes the
regulator of her own internal world.

Andrew's situation has got more elements in it than that of a child
in a sweet shop. The coach is not a parent to the client but the regulatory
mechanisms that are in use are exactly the same as in parent–child interactions
even if brought into play differently. And the essence of the coaching situation
is exactly the same as for the child spending money. There are competing
choices to be made. Underlying the thought processes are feelings, none of
which give sufficient clarity for a clear course of action – unlike the choices that
were made about Andrew and family not going to Africa where the clarity of
Andrew's wife's feelings and choices amplified and justified his.

Motivational processes

Jennifer

Jennifer told us she had done a PhD in cell biology twenty-five years ago, but
had not gone on to use her PhD directly because an international consulting
firm had offered her a great deal more money for her analytical skills than the

pharmaceutical companies were offering for newly-doctored scientists to be at a research bench.

Five years ago she left consulting and trained as an executive coach but had recently begun to feel a bit intellectually understimulated; and though still much engaged by the practical challenges of coaching was slightly regretting not having stayed in a scientific field that, over the following quarter-century, had become one of the most exciting places to be in science. But she had recently come across the fact that the brain sciences were beginning to edge their way into the corporate world through executive coaching.

Suddenly two parts of Jennifer's life began to come together with new potentials opening up for reviving old knowledge that had been exciting to her at the time. She could see that they could come together with prospects of turning them, in an emergent way, to a different account than she could ever have imagined might have happened when she made the choice to abandon neuroscience to go into management consultancy and then executive coaching.

That has a whole different set of actionable possibilities in it than the scenario we described with Simon – *because the feelings are different.* In consequence the motivational processes are different. Jennifer has no sense of doubt. Quite the contrary. After an afternoon's introductory session on coaching in a brain-based way her eyes are alight as oxytocin floods her brain – a fact that she laughingly tells us she knows is happening – and she can see an old love of brain science coming back into her life. The energy from action potentials is pouring out of her. She is wondering where and how and how soon she can pursue her surge of reviving interest. Attachment emotions in circuits of the brain that have long been understimulated are waiting to be harnessed in creative ways. As she said: 'I feel like one happy bunny this afternoon'.

Simon and Andrew and Jennifer all evidence 'wondering' as a way of framing inner experience. In each case, though, the quality of the wondering that starts from startle/surprise is differently constituted through different mixes of the basic emotions. With Jennifer and Simon they are conscious of clear connections to life events, though the outcomes for each are different. With Andrew there are more complex issues around, connected to a decision that is apparently more far-reaching in its implications for him than whether or not to get involved in applied neuroscience. And there are also questions for the coach about how Andrew goes about making decisions anyway.

The mind

But all three are bending their minds to the task of sorting out what seems to be the best course of action and it is time to consider what this chimereal thing called 'the mind' might be.

The applied neurosciences have started developing two distinct tracks of thought. One comes from the corporate field and one comes from the clinical field.

The corporate field is perhaps best evidenced in the emerging work and impact of *The NeuroLeadership Institute*, started by David Rock and Al Ringleb some five years ago. It is avowedly trying to bring together the field practices of executive coaching and the laboratory work of neuroscientists. It proposes that there are four domains of leadership to which the brain sciences might especially be applied:

- Decision-making
- Problem-solving
- Emotional regulation
- Collaboration and facilitating change

It relies upon the laboratory work of what are usually called the **cognitive social neurosciences**.

Cognitive social neuroscience

The usual experimental method that cognitive social neuroscientists use is mapping what happens in the brain by using fMRI or other brain imaging techniques. An experimental situation is created and is tracked for its effect(s) upon the brain. An elegant experiment of such a kind is one on social pain by Naomi Eisenberger a social psychologist at UCLA, and colleagues (2005), which set out to start understanding what happens in the brain as a consquence of social rejection.

Lying in a scanner, the experimental subject is shown a short cartoon film of three pairs of hand passing a ball between them. The hands are arranged on the screen as an inverted triangle, and the experimental subject is told that the hands at the bottom of the screen are theirs. For a short time the ball is passed between the three pairs of hands of three (apparent) people happily playing ball, sometimes in one direction, sometimes in another, but all involved. It is an experimental situation that seems to provoke a high degree of identification between the subject and feeling involved in what is happening on the screen.

After a short time the experimental conditions change. The hands at the bottom of the screen, with which the experimental subject has been identifying, no longer receive the ball. It is being passed only between the two upper pair of hands. The lower pair of hands has been excluded. The experimental subject has no power to alter the conditions on the screen, just to experience whatever is experienced.

What Eisenberger has shown is that, in this simulation of social rejection, areas of the brain that are closely associated with the areas involved in physical pain become active. It is as if social pain and physical pain are functionally similar in the brain. We can observe also that a difference between the two is that endorphins do not rush in to quell the emotional pain as they do with physical pain. So social pain can be remembered and rehearsed again and again.

This kind of work is a good example of what has been a long tradition in the neurosciences. It is called *localization*. The neuroscientist's interest is to work out, in a systematic mapping way, which bit of the brain functions when some specific event happens. And does that happen on repeated occasions, and does it happen to all brains? In such a way a working model of the brain might eventually be built up from the enormous amount of different observations and experiments. Social cognitive neuroscientists are especially interested in how we, as human beings, see and interpret our world and which parts of the brain do that.

A working model of the mind

This kind of work is somewhat different from the work of Daniel Siegel, also at UCLA, who twenty years ago in the early days of the modern neuroscience imaging revolution started developing what he has called '**interpersonal neurobiology**'. A child and adult psychiatrist with a long-term special interest in attachment theory, Siegel has been particularly interested in trying to construct a working model of the mind. His interest is not so much in the detail of which bit of the brain lights up when something happens, though that is always in the background of his thinking, but how the whole thing works as an integrated system. He has suggested, in a great imaginative leap, that it is a property of the physical structure of the brain to organize itself in such a way that it is continuously managing information, energy and relationship. That is how he characterizes the mind.

Draw or imagine an equilateral triangle sitting on its base. The left-hand slope is labelled 'information'; the right-hand side 'energy'; and the base is labelled 'relationship'.

We cannot emphasize too much what a remarkable suggestion this is. Psychology has previously left 'mind' to be the intellectual domain of philosophers: and indeed there is a rich literature to do with theory of mind. But none of it arrives at working, applicable conclusions. Freud, who was fascinated by the mind constructed, as we have already observed, a working model that is essentially wrong though it has sunk deeply into the Western intellectual tradition. But Siegel has got there.

Energy
The physical source of energy is well known – oxygen and glucose coursing through the blood provide the food that any physical structure in the body needs to keep it functioning. How the brain shunts it around to where it is needed is still something of a mystery.

The brain itself functions off about 20 watts of energy which is, considering its size (two-to-three per cent of a person's body weight), a disproportionate amount of the 70–80 watts or so that the whole body works off; though it is perhaps not disproportionate when considering its central task in organizing the whole of the body's systems. The brain is certainly one of the most continuously energy-hungry organs in the body and is vulnerable to its energy supply being cut off. Ten minutes of failure can produce irreversible brain damage. When one particular part of the brain needs more energy, the brain does not simply create more. It shifts available supply to where it is needed, like a squad of soldiers being sent somewhere else. That much *is* known, and it has some interesting consequences.

There is a part of the right-hand-side frontal area of the brain, a little way inside on the surface of the fissure that separates the two halves of the brain – called, the **right ventro-lateral prefrontal cortex** – that is especially involved in creative integration. At the end of 2011 Tobias Egner of Duke University demonstrated that this area of the brain is also important in sorting out conflict-driven adjustments in cognitive control; which is about situations where there are competing demands for attention.

As a broad generalization, think of the right-hand side of the brain as being particularly concerned with things that are new (the where and the why of perception) and the left-hand side of the brain is concerned with the what that is known. Then in executive environments, where senior people are having to respond a great deal of the time to the *un*known, it would be reasonable to assume that Egner's experimental findings are important; because the unknown and competing demands will both require sorting out.

Now add in the fact that the brain can only shunt its energy supply around and not generate more, and think of a situation in which your client is stressed, day by day. It might be a major complex project that is going wrong, it might be a poor upward relationship with a demanding boss who makes no resource time for discussion yet rages at the outcome of whatever is done. Whatever the situation you are imagining, let it be of the stressful kind that makes for early morning waking, not looking forward to work, and a growing feeling of incapacity.

But let us understand not just the fact of the experience (whilst remembering that stress thresholds are immensely variable from person to person). Consider what is happening in the brain. The energy that is being used to manage everything concerned with the stress is not available to the area of the brain that seems to have the capacity to sort out problems. The squad can only be in one place at a time. The more the boss shouts, the more the adaptive system closes down because the energy is being diverted to the parts of the brain – hypothalamic pituitary adrenal axis among others – to hope, to cope, to survive. The more stress increases as the complex project gets bogged down the less effective are the solutions.

In both cases – and an infinite number more in everyday corporate life – the outcomes are the exact opposite of what would be most useful. The capacity to wonder gets switched off in favour of survival. The capacity to be adaptive gets shut down. So the brain's best bet under conditions of stress is to do what it knows best – which is to regulate everything for survival. Early-morning waking/poor sleep? *Go on to automatic pilot at work.* Cannot bear the sight of the boss? *Do what has to be done despite the dread.* Feeling exhausted? *Long for the weekend.* Weekend arrives? *Cannot relax and family suffer.* The point is that under these conditions your client can tell himself over and over again how things *ought* to be but cannot will them the way he wants them.

But what of the other two components of mind – information and relationship?

Information

It has been characteristic of the later part of the twentieth century and increasingly so into this one that we have become swamped with information. The brain needs energy to process it. You will know from all kinds of personal experience how tiredness affects the capacity to deal with information. Tiredness is only another set of chemical conditions. Because it is familiar we take for granted reductions in cognitive skill associated with increased tiredness. But if large amounts of energy in the brain are being used in processing too much information, once again the creative and adaptive resources are not available for being well used. Even worse, the activity becomes mind-less, which is once again the opposite of what organizations want.

Relationship

As for relationship, it is profound – which is why it was especially emphasized in Chapter 2 and will be more so in Chapter 6. Between people the resonating capacity of the emotional system to create the conditions, via the amygdala, under which the brain functions at its best are extraordinary. Equally powerful are the conditions under which the resonating transmission of emotions can make another person's brain respond only in survival mode. And as there is no communication without emotion being involved, the effectiveness of relationship becomes key to both the managing of energy and the understanding of information – if meaning cannot be assigned to the information it becomes meaningless. And the basis of meaning is emotion.

So your client comes to you with a mind that has the potential for these three particular and perhaps special components of information, energy and relationship being in a continuous dynamic relationship one with another. The coaching task to create the conditions for personal development and growth is to make sure they are. And the key to that process is relationship. And first of all, executive coach, your relationship with yourself.

Summary

'Wondering' is one manifestation of the basic emotion of surprise. It is invaluable as a means of engaging a client in the beginnings of the processes that will create and consolidate change. All the eight basic emotions create energy. They have the capacity to create new networks in the brain and are the source of motivation. One way in which the activities of the brain consolidate themselves is in the working of the Mind, in which information, energy and relationship combine together to make experience not only cohesive but coherent.

The practical statement you will almost certainly be making at this stage is: 'Well, that is all well and good and perhaps I agree with what you are saying. But *what* exactly do I have to do? I am a busy coach, time is precious, I do have some worries of my own about performing well as a coach and making sure the deliverables I am supposed to be delivering are delivered. What *exactly* do I have to do?'

Good. You are wondering. Here's a starting point for what to do.

5 Neurobehavioural Modelling (NBM)

Putting knowledge to use

This chapter introduces **Neurobehavioural Modelling** (NBM), a way we have developed that begins to structure the new brain sciences into an integrated body of knowledge to put into use in the practice of coaching.

One of the many inhibitors of new developments in organizations is the demand for numbers and for evidence. But new developments have to begin somewhere and there are times at such beginnings where numbers and evidence are neither possible, practical nor desirable. In new beginnings things have to be *imagined*. Intuitive leaps are made that have a strong basis in thought and sense even if still light on actual experience. They take advantage of that extraordinary property of the human brain to bring together in new ways the information that is contained within it, and through that synthesis to make new connections and new sense: and then to test these out on others to see if it makes new sense for them too.

That is what we are doing here. Neurobehavioural Modelling is such a beginning. It has behind it a good deal of working knowledge of the brain plus hundreds of hours between us of coaching, clinical and organizational consulting experience. In an empirical sense it is unproven, though not untested. It is an initial statement of what a coaching intervention would look like if you start from what is increasingly known about the brain, rather than starting from what coaching practice says and then adding on bits of knowledge about the brain.

This is an important distinction. Should coaching simply seek to explain and reinforce what it already knows by adding in, when convenient, what the brain sciences are discovering? Or should we coaches be trying to develop new forms of thinking and practice out of applying the new brain sciences? We have chosen the latter course of action – not because we have any brief for wanting to revise the whole of coaching practice. Far from it – existing practice is a still an important element. It would indeed be foolish not to incorporate what, for any coach, is tried, tested and well-known (even if coaching also generally lacks the evidence-based validations that are so beloved of many organizations). What we do want to do, however, with existing coaching skills and knowledge is to recontextualize them. The starting point is knowing how the brain works and developing practice from that vantage point. In such a way we hope to encourage you to be faithful to all that you are learning about the brain so that this can discipline your practice, develop your insights, and make new knowledge practically available in the service of your client. Even if that is initially uncomfortable to do, we think you will find it fascinating and hugely rewarding. And there can be little doubt that the twenty-first century will be the time when the brain sciences inform us about human behaviour in a way that was unimaginable twenty-five years ago. So you will be developing your professionalism on the leading edge of where developments are bound to go.

Many professions go through stages where new knowledge requires a shift in practice. Once it has been made, the shift – if it proves to have been well-founded and essentially right in concept – becomes self-evident, even if it is not always exactly right in fine detail at the beginning. An understanding of germs and how infections were transmitted caused a revolution in nursing and the standards of hygiene in surgery, for instance. Prior to such knowledge being available the practices that were clearly right, subsequently, were never even considered. So we think it will be the same for coaching with regard to the brain sciences. We also think that, in parallel, there will be a huge impact from the brain sciences upon the way Human Resources understands, constructs and justifies its organizational role in the future, though that time may still be some way off.

The impetus for formalizing NBM came, curiously, from Vietnam. In the spring of 2011 one of us had been invited to speak in Da Nang at a mental health conference convened by the five countries of the sub-Mekong Region – Thailand, Myanmar, Vietnam, Cambodia and Laos. Out of that came a request from the Vietnamese delegation to create a three-day teaching programme on how to use the modern brain sciences in psychotherapy. Although the outline of NBM practice in coaching had been formulated a couple of years previously, and had been in systematic but exploratory use in executive coaching, the formalizing of it had not taken place until this request to see how it applied to the practice of psychotherapy. That formalizing came from executive coaching experience and some continuing clinical experience – an unusual example, perhaps, of the executive coaching field informing the clinical, rather than vice versa.

Chapter 10 elaborates the principles of Neurobehavioural Modelling, using case material that has been developed throughout the book. At this stage of beginning to think about the brain and how to put that knowledge into use we set out six propositions that, if you understand what is meant by each one, you can rehearse to yourself, and use with clients. These will give you as complete a frame of reference as you need to start trying out your knowledge about the brain with clients. The six include, at number 4, the three fundamental propositions of the first three chapters.

Imagine you are at a dinner party, or in front of a prospective client, and you are asked what you do, and you say that you are interested in the brain and using that knowledge in executive coaching, and the person says then tell me something about the brain: knowing these six propositions will demonstrate that you really do seem to know something that is both interesting and coherent. This chapter sets out to equip you to deal professionally with that situation.

1. The brain is an integrated system with many specialized highly-differentiated areas

The cognitive social neurosciences tend to focus their research attention on specific areas of the brain – what is called '**localization**'. 'What happens in the brain when this or that happens to a person?' is the underlying key question that keeps many labs busy. But, following Daniel Siegel's work in developing interpersonal neurobiology, executive coaching might, we suggest, best develop practice through an understanding of how the whole system works.

An unfortunate obstacle to this is that no-one yet knows how the whole system does work. That is the state of the science. What is possible though is to make some imaginative but well-founded jumps and assumptions, and create a whole systems model that can be useful in practice as the model itself goes on developing.

Think of a twenty-first-century motor car. In some senses such a car was entirely inherent in the design of the first automobile. From Karl Benz in 1886 onwards, steps were taken around a central concept that was essentially right (though Benz had behind him a tradition of steam engines and the designs for them that goes back to at least 1672). Adopting the whole idea of a self-propelled, controllable, steerable vehicle containing a combustion engine running on a volatile substance called petroleum, that could carry human beings at a speed faster and for longer duration than that of a horse, proved to be a viable concept.

One-hundred-and-twenty-five years of technical and stylistic innovation have not altered that essential concept. It still defines a motor car. Equally, but oppositely, as noted earlier, more than a hundred years of twentieth-century descriptive psychology have not established a scientifically viable concept of what underpins human behaviour – a scientifically-derived model of a whole person. The hope now is that the brain sciences are moving in that direction.

NBM is a start in setting out to take what is known at this stage, and to establish the working beginnings of a neuroscientifically-derived model for coaching. It starts from daring to think of an integrated model as best we have it at the moment – a brain that manages to get highly differentiated parts functioning together in a single whole – and being true to that model in practice. Siegel's proposal that the appearance of mind is a function of the way the brain organizes itself to manage information, energy and relationships is a special element of this.

2. The brain manages the inputs and the outputs from the five senses

This is the brain's essential task. The world out there provides the data. Each of the five senses – touch, taste, smell, hearing and vision – are waiting to be stimulated individually or in any combination. Specialized areas of the brain deal with each, while aspects of the whole brain integrate them in a continuous organized process of making sense.

Some people talk of a sixth sense, which is to do with the processes of maintaining balance (equilibrium) and a sense of body position (proprioception). Both have well-defined areas of the brain linked to them and linked to each other, but they are not parts of everyday conscious awareness in a way that the five main senses are. The difference is that the data for the sixth sense comes from 'in here' rather than 'out there'. The sixth sense is most readily observed when it goes wrong – giddiness or sudden loss of balance, for instance – though in sports coaching it is of profound importance. But in many ways it is not a sense that will generally be of particular concern in executive coaching, though we do have one instance of where it was key to the way a coach saw, without understanding why, that a client had changed.

Maggie

A coach in supervision agreed with her supervisor that a managing director she was coaching ought to have his contract terminated. The coach felt his level of disrespect for her and all that they had agreed to try and accomplish in coaching was being systematically demolished. The fact that it was adversely affecting her own sense of well-being was also something that she had considered. This was the first time in five years of coaching that such a situation had arisen for her. Indeed, it was this kind of behaviour that had brought the managing director into coaching in the first place, at his chairman's request. That she had not managed to change anything was an acute sense of disappointment to her.

Two days later the supervisor took a telephone call from the coach. 'I want to tell you I failed to make the contract termination we agreed on', she said.

Something in the buoyant, slightly triumphant, tone of voice left the supervisor immediately intrigued. 'Tell me', was all he said.

'Well', said the coach, 'when I arrived at the floor his office is on I saw him walking down the corridor a little way ahead of me. The moment I saw him he looked different. It was in his walk. He looked straighter, somehow. So when we got into the session and I was a bit hesitant to make the speech I had been dreading anyway he said, straight away: "I know I've been giving you a hard time in the sessions we have had so far. It took me a while to understand what you were on about and why I should change. I've been pretty successful in my career this far, and I think the chairman's a bit of an old fusspot as you know. But last night my daughter said to me, when we were having supper, that she thought I was so much nicer when I relaxed and why couldn't I be like that more of the time. You know she brings the best out in me anyway. And I suddenly thought that that was what you have been going on about, really. Between the two of you I understand. Bloody women! But I thought if maybe I was nicer then I would relax. So from today I'm going to be nicer. Will that do?"'

'So what did you say?' said the supervisor to a perceptive coach.

'What was there worth saying?', said the coach. 'I hugged him. I can't tell you how surprised we both were. It just happened. I embarrassed us both, a bit, but in a nice way. Then he said he also wanted to extend the contract, just to keep him on track for a while because he thinks he might slip back. He said after all he hasn't got this far by being especially nice, though I told him I always thought it was in him to be different. And he said really he agreed, only it had to come from him. And I couldn't disagree with that.'

3. The brain both regulates and is regulated by its emotional system

The emotional system serves the function of not only creating meaning by attaching feelings to experience but also of being the source of the energy that underlies motivation. Remember 'e-motion' – energy transformed into directed action is what motivation is about.

The key function of an effective, continuous, adult relationship upon the immature brain of the infant is to develop, bit by bit in the infant's brain, the capacity to regulate its own emotional, and so its behavioural, system. The relationship does that, in part, by actually stimulating the physical growth of the brain in areas concerned with social recognition and social interaction. It takes a long time, right up through adolescence, with a wide variety of social influencers adding on to the original parental input, to get the whole system effective.

This complex tuning of one (immature/undeveloped) brain by another (mature/developed) brain forms the basis of all effective social interaction for the whole of a life. It is what makes the brain continuously subject, throughout life, to the impact of relationship in all its forms. Though in coaching the two brains are physically mature the same mechanism of emotional regulation is continuously at work and is the basis of NBM. It is the basis of behavioural change that sticks and is key to effective coaching.

What attachment research shows again and again is that the way the brain gets organized emotionally – as a consequence of its early emotional experiences – is what makes any one individual the person they become. The emotional system defines the associative circuitry of that individual's uniquely organized brain. This is the sense-making mechanism within the person. An event attached to emotion(s) creates meaning. It gets distributed up into the cortex and forms the beginning of knowledge related to that event. There is no template about how it *should* be. All the brain knows is how it *is*. This is why real change within the individual is so difficult to establish and maintain. The *idea* of change might be easily agreed upon; the purpose and direction of change too. But the *actuality* of change requires a rewiring, in part, of the way the brain in its emotional and feeling system is already wired. That is what coaching is about – making new connections in the brain

Look at change from the brain's point of view for a moment. Suppose you are being required to change. Your brain is the brain that has got you to where you are today. Much the safest bet would be to go on being the same. Not only are lots of new circuits and connections an effort to establish, but there is no proof, prior to change happening, that the change will be better than what has already been pretty useful so far.

This is exactly what so many change consultants describe as the perpetual frustration of their professional lives. The need for change seems obvious, but establishing that change is so difficult.

But what about those individuals who do embrace change in a whole-hearted and effective way? What of their brains? There are two observations that can be made at this stage.

The first is that there will be some individuals whose brain circuitry has developed in such a way that they are naturally and spontaneously excited and intrigued by new-ness. They naturally and positively *like* change – an accident of their own developmental history. Such individuals are well-adapted to situations where change is afoot and indeed change is their normal preferred state. It would be interesting to conduct a study to see how many people in change consultancies have a developmental history that embraces change and makes it an ordinary part of their everyday life. It would also be interesting to distinguish among such individuals those for whom the *hope* of change that was never fulfilled was part of their developmental history.

The Labour prime minister, Gordon Brown, made much play of his own adversity in life when unsuccessfully campaigning in the 2010 General Election. His argument ran that as his knowledge and adolescent experience of adversity were aligned to tumultuous and adverse election circumstances so it meant that there was an affinity between himself and the current time that made him a singularly appropriate leader.

What he failed to inform the electorate about was how to get *out* of adversity. He seemed to enjoy the struggle with adversity without being able to define a way for reaching the other side. Among many other factors that lost him the election it was clear that being part of his continuing struggle did not appeal to a majority of the electorate.

The second observation is that the emotional patterning within any one person's brain will have different value in different contexts. In a commercial setting where change is high on the agenda, a brain that is stimulated into positive action by the demand for change may have high value, but not so in another context. 'Leadership' is, in part, so difficult to define for the same reason. It is a contextual matter. Different times require different brains.

4. The brain is the organ for making sense, for managing relationships, and is a remarkable neurochemical factory

Previously explored separately, we have put them together here at the centre of this group of six propositions as you extend your own internalized model of the brain. This is because they are the most basic part of the knowledge needed and lie at the heart of any understanding of how the social brain works.

5. The brain has no original templates, only possibilities

This proposition is true for the brain when it comes into the world, but less and less true as development through childhood, into adolescence, and then to early adult life takes place. Indeed, it is the function of development to make templates and to start limiting possibilities.

The brain has no sense that it 'ought' to be of any particular kind, any more than a pile of bricks knows what kind of house they might construct. Each brain becomes unique. Most coaches 'know' that each client is unique and different; but what we especially want you to be aware of is that in knowing that fact you do not nevertheless try to understand and evaluate the client through the prisms of your own templates.

Of course each brain *is* pretty much exactly like yours from the point of view of structure and function – just as every other grown-up person of your gender on the planet is pretty much like you from the point of view of their essential physicality; but so completely *un*like you in the detail of how that physicality presents itself to the world that you would be surprised to meet someone who closely resembled you in any way at all.

So it is with the brain, whose properties are much less easy to observe. This is the mystery inherent in the coaching process. The person who comes for coaching is profoundly different from you. It is getting into that difference that creates successful coaching – though it is not to be construed as *difference* (from me) but as uniqueness in the other person. *I* (the coach) am not the reference point for the definition of the client. And yet. . . . The fact is that you, the coach, can only know the other person through your own frame of reference, through your own templates.

That has implications for developing the right templates within yourself – new ways of making sense. That, of course, is what learning is about all the time – whatever it is you are learning. On this occasion what we are encouraging you to do – and what you have already started to do perhaps, by reading this book thus far – is to create templates – new pathways in your own cortical system – that let you look at and understand your client at the highest possible resolution of understanding. This becomes practicable as your focus sharpens into understanding your client's templates – experiences and frames of reference – without testing them against your own. In such a way you will begin to accomplish what we regard as one of the most fundamental of coaching skills – being able to look at the world through your client's eyes. This is not about being empathetic. It is about *being* the person, in part, because you can see how the world looks from your client's perspective. You do that through understanding the emotional system driving your client's behaviour. Perhaps this is the absolutely fundamental professional task of the coach – to know your client as he or she *is,* not as he or she is supposed to be.

This is quite a challenge. As a coach you may have to factor in the organization's frames of reference and specifications about what is expected of the person you are coaching. The trouble with this prescriptive organizational demand, from a brain-based point of view, is that specifying how someone *is* to *be* massively limits that person's adaptive capacity to pursue goals adaptively. In much modern organizational practice means and ends have become completely confused, to the extent that means have become ends in themselves. One organization approached one of us with the request to create a workshop for establishing higher levels of trust among senior supervisors in the organization. After discussion the request was declined. It was apparent that the organization did not understand that trust was a complex state that could only flow from the leadership within the organization, not a commodity subject to transactional rules. The personal development specialist making the request did not understand that dirty water upstream can't be dealt with by trying to make clean water downstream: and he was unwilling to explore with the CEO the damaging effects throughout the organization of the way low trust within the Board manifested itself throughout the organization.

Edward

Edward, an accountant-turned-management consultant, was invited to join an international firm to develop a particular section of the renewable energy market. From a standing start he built up, over four years, a highly successful practice within the firm. In consequence he started attracting senior management's particular attention. The Management Committee began to wonder how they could maximize on Edward's increasing success, with the intention of creating cross-selling opportunities for other parts of the firm. Management decided to establish an 'energy consortium', with five partners from various aspects of the firm coming together to pursue the stated intentions that were very broadly drawn. At the same time Edward had been offered six months' coaching as part of the firm's standard practice for new partners.

Edward had had little experience of collaborative interaction in his life. He was the only child of an academic philosopher father who was completely absorbed in his own intellectual pursuits and nearly twenty years older than Edward's mother. She had had no pretensions to learning in any way at all but ran a comfortable home for the two men in her life. Edward was born and lived in the same house until he left it to go away to university, by which time his father was about to retire formally while maintaining an emeritus relationship with his old department.

Edward had little memory of any vivid events in his childhood. Strong emotions were not welcome as part of the currency of family life. In the days before computer games, reading was much approved of. One thing he did remember, though, was being taken to see the open coffin of his mother's Irish father when he died, he and his mother having travelled to Ireland for the funeral. Edward was eleven at the time.

For Edward, life in a small university town as he grew up was lived, it seemed, within highly predictable routines and little change in the emotional tone of anything. He did his best, and did well at school. Birthdays were not celebrated at any level of intensity. Christmas was something he remembered most strongly as being an occasion of slight upset in routines and surprise that his father would don the paper hat from a cracker until, generally, it slipped off and was then left alone. Edward learnt in his later teenage years that his mother always went to midnight mass on Christmas Eve, though there was no family religious practice otherwise. Christmas Eve was not the kind of time of excitement when a child might well be awake until midnight and beyond.

Edward's strongest memory of his father, as he was growing up, was of him seeming slightly embarrassed around him, as if he were perpetually surprised that Edward was anything to do with him. Edward had wondered, when he was at university, what the circumstances of own birth were. With some simple detective work he established that he was conceived before his parents' marriage, though it was a discovery that he kept entirely to himself. By the time of the events that began this brief account of Edward's life his father had acquired a senile dementia, and his mother's life was constrained by being his constant carer. In any event they lived a good distance away from the London of Edward's demanding career and they had little contact.

In coaching sessions Edward talked about how stressful he found the 'energy consortium' group in his firm. It seemed to him that the firm was creating conditions that were designed to dilute his success by wanting others to join in somehow. One particularly vocal and assertive member of the group had just come back from five years of establishing the firm's offices in Singapore and was looking to rebuild a London client base for himself. Edward found him predatory of his own client relationships.

Whatever the merits or otherwise of the firm's energy consortium idea, Edward had absolutely no experience – and hence no templates – with which to adapt to the circumstances that he felt were being imposed detrimentally upon him. He began to ruminate in the early mornings about making a constructive dismissal case against the firm; about having such a row with the one predatory partner that he, the other partner, would be forced to leave the firm; or that he would simply not attend the monthly consortium meetings and see what happened. None of these were likely to be effective strategies, but all are typical of a situation where, in the absence of adaptive templates arising from prior experience, what had previously been a thoroughly adequate strategy proves in changing circumstances to be so no longer.

Like many advisory professionals, Edward had been trained in a way that put a high premium upon knowledge and technical expertise and almost none on interpersonal skills. As a junior accountant working his way up a firm he had in those days been a partner's delight; industrious, keen to get things right and so appearing to be good at taking critical comment, focused on deadlines, and accurate. It had got him where he had got to. By any standards his brain was doing a good job for him. The templates he had developed had got him here – a salaried partner in a very well-known international consulting firm at an age that was slightly younger than the average age across firms of this kind for his level. But when the rules of the game changed it exposed the fact that he had little interpersonal adaptive capacity.

Edward lived with his girlfriend in a relationship of some six years. She was in marketing and was as ebullient and outgoingly imaginative as Edward was reserved and predictable. Edward said they each enjoyed the other's differences. He calmed her and she took him into experiences – like going to Glastonbury soon after they first met – that opened doors for him he had never been through before. He said he couldn't confess to always liking what his girlfriend set up – Glastonbury had been particularly muddy – but he appreci-ated the experiences. He had also been surprised at the kudos his Glastonbury expedition had given him within the firm he was in at the time. He was happy being led into experiences of life and was continuously quietly surprised that his girlfriend stayed with him.

When asked who else in his life had been surprised at the other person who was there, Edward was startled to observe that he seemed to be repli-cating his father's pattern. He wondered if his father had been more delighted with him than he had been able to show. Although, in transactional analysis terms, looking at Edward's present life, the stage was different and the charac-ters had changed, the emotional plot of his family life was essentially the same at this period of his adult life. Seeing that patterning helped Edward to see how much the brain works in ways that are not usually brought into conscious thought.

So Edward's life had, thus far, both created and limited his possibilities. That is true for everyone, but the specifics of how it is true are unique to every individual. We shall come back to Edward when sustainable change is central to our concerns.

It used to be thought, until recently, and as a result of the Freudian view of what psychic life was about, that poor or absent memory about childhood such as Edward had ('childhood amnesia', it was called) between the ages of three and adolescence was indicative of repression of untoward events. Many psychotherapists would still ascribe to the event of seeing his grandfather dead the lack of memory for much of his childhood. But we now know that this is not at all the way the development of the brain and memory works.

It seems that there are two elements that are necessary to establish effective childhood memories for later adult recall. The first is that the part of the brain that organizes sequential events has to have developed. That is a maturational process that may not establish itself properly until eight or nine years of age. The second is that events have to happen with enough emotional tone in them for them to form memory traces with sufficient energy to be accessible to subsequent regeneration of the memory.

And finally:

6. The brain hates change

This hardly needs more observation than has already been made – except of course to remind you of the paradox that the person who has a brain that is wired for change is no exception to this rule! Such a person also wants to go on being the same – though in a change-demand environment they may have a first-mover advantage on many occasions.

So these six propositions are the elements that you need to have continuously in mind when approaching coaching from a brain-based vantage point. Then what is needed is a structure within which to use that knowledge.

What we are calling Neurobehavioural Modelling, NBM, is a first formulation of how to use the new and emerging brain sciences in coaching systematically. This chapter has been about the framework within which to think and talk about the brain and organize your own accumulating information. What comes next is the detail of how to proceed.

The formal definition of NBM is:

> NBM is the means by which an executive coach, who has a working knowledge of the brain and mind, interacts with a client [individual

or group, brain(s) to brain(s)] for the contractually-agreed purposes of creating (structural) change in (the brain of) the client so that –

- behaviour changes
- the Self is modified, and
- the gains made are consolidated over time into lasting and sustainable change

That is a challenging statement. We have been challenging ourselves with it over the past three years. The next chapter begins to answer the questions that immediately arise from such a statement. 'Just what is meant by "structural change" and "the Self"?'

Summary

This chapter has introduced Neurobehavioural Modelling (NBM) as a framework to guide coaches in using a working knowledge of the brain for creating change and facilitating development in a client. It sees the fundamental coaching skill as being one that uses the coaching relationship to create the possibility of establishing new networks in the client's brain that are then manifest in all kinds of behaviours that also need consolidating over time.

In order to define the knowledge base an executive coach needs to have in order to practise responsibly from a brain-based point of view, six propositions have been outlined that together encapsulate a working knowledge of a whole model of the way the brain works at what is still an early stage in the science of knowing how the brain works.

6 Behavioural change that sticks

It is relationship that is at the heart of effective coaching. But what gets effective coaching to endure as a permanent shift in the other person is practice, practice, practice. Relationship triggers the possibility of real change but it is practice that embeds it.

At the end of Chapter 5 we defined the essence of Neurobehavioural Modelling as being 'the means by which an executive coach who has a working knowledge of the brain and mind interacts with a client [individual or group, brain(s) to brain(s)] for the contractually-agreed purposes of creating (structural) change in (the brain of) the client'. That definition is also the basis of the contractual relationship that needs to exist between coach and client for brain-to-brain coaching to be not only effective but ethical.

Set in brackets in this definition and basic contractual specification are those parts of it that, if you really want to become a brain-informed and brain-based coach, require special attention. It is intended that you should make conscious to yourself, and equally conscious to your client, just what it is you are about.

The fact of the matter is, whenever you sit down with a client and engage in effective coaching, changing the brain *is* what you are about. There can be no effective coaching without the brains of coach and client being engaged together for the deliberate purpose of making change in the client's brain. By that we mean not just thinking together, but influencing each other, tuned to each other, resonating. It is a central argument of this book that this can, indeed should, be done by design, not just by default. Both coach and client need to know what they are letting themselves in for. It is about deliberately changing the client's brain *in the direction(s) that the client says change is wanted*. And behavioural change means changing the flow in some part(s) of the brain's neural network.

Complexity

The complexity of the brain is something that we have passed over relatively lightly – eighty billion cells each with the capacity for ten thousand connections. But brought down to a very small level, every cubic millimetre of the cortex contains around one billion synapses. Natural development of the brain is a highly organized and complex process. The deliberate changing of that organized complexity is something that should be done with as much finesse as possible. At the present state of knowledge what we can do now will look clumsy in ten years' time. But arguably it is better than the hit-and-miss methods of uninformed happenstance.

Development and adaptation

A 2012 report in *Science Now* by Jon Cohen describes how it is becoming understood that, genetically, the human brain actually wires itself up very slowly through the developmental period of childhood into adolescence. Compared with our near relatives, chimpanzees and macaques, with which we have 98.8 per cent similarity in our genes, synaptic connections in the prefrontal cortex are made unhurriedly in humans.

Whether this is the result or the cause of the long period of dependency that human infants have upon their parents is not known. But the consequence of this slow wiring process is that humans develop much greater adaptive **plasticity** than do our near primate relatives. It may also be the case, though, that once this adaptive plasticity has established its connections it is quite resistant to change. And the interconnectedness of language development in humans is another big variable in the complexity of the associative pathways that are being made. These observations serve to remind coaches that it is wise to be humble when engaging professionally with the brain. And part of that humbleness might be for coaches to prepare themselves as well as they possibly can for the task they are taking on of being involved with the changing of someone else's brain. It is a responsibility that cannot properly be ignored.

To illustrate this, remember the description in Chapter 3 of what was happening to Jim where he was left in a situation with cortisol flooding his system and his adaptive capacities being wrecked by stress. His ways of dealing with this were part of a pattern that was causing concern to others inside his organization and creating a dysfunctional marriage. Knowing this a coach could be certain that what Jim was evidencing was not just the outbursts of a stressed man but well-established templates working in a way that, in his present environment, were seriously counter-productive, however productive they had been when first set up.

It would seem to make sense – though this is not something that evolutionary science will ever prove one way or the other – that the brain would never do something obviously self-destructive. That is to say, when persisting patterns of behaviours first get set up they must have had adaptive value *otherwise they would not have established themselves*. So when it is apparent that the behaviour is maladaptive what has changed is the context. This is another way of reflecting on the TA rubric that, with established patterns, what can be observed is that the stage changes, the characters change, but the plot stays essentially the same.

So in a coaching context there is little to be gained by trying to get Jim to *stop* what he is doing – it is part of him. If Jim's coach starts with the assumption that Jim should stop what he is doing then he is being asked, effectively, to stop being himself. The whole of his system will resist such a request.

New pathways

What has to be done is to invite Jim to decide whether or not he wishes to use the energy that seems to be creating maladaptive behaviours to find new pathways – new networks, new attachments – within the structures that already exist: or experiment with creating new networks if there is nothing apparent on which to build. If that can be accomplished the old patterns become redundant; but the stop is a consequence of establishing the new patterns. There is never anything to be gained in trying to instruct the brain what *not* to do. It has no mechanisms for that. It wants to know *what* to do.

The start point is the assumption that the behaviours Jim is evidencing are widely diffused in the networks of his brain, with infinite connections of which neither he nor his coach could possibly have any awareness at all. Yet if his coach creates the conditions under which Jim can get his brain to cooperate with what he ostensibly wants to do (presuming he really is in coaching wholeheartedly and not just to satisfy the demands of his chairman) then his brain can be trusted to do the work to create the pathways that would underpin his new behaviours. That is what the brain is very good at *once engaged* – the client's brain will do the work if the coach's brain can create the conditions.

So how does it do that to create change that sticks?

Resonance

It is useful to have, ticking away in the back of your mind, what you know of the amygdala, the emotions, and the mind. You are managing all of those in yourself and, by **resonance**, in your client for the whole of every session.

The whole system controlled by the amygdala is effectively a transmitter as well as a receiver. The amygdala of a client pick up everything that is going on in the coach's brain, assess the emotional loading of all stimuli, and so make the emotional significance of what is going on in the coach's brain apparent to the client. That, through the efficacy of the coaching relationship, mobilizes the energy systems within the client's mind to process both the self-generated and the coach-generated data (information) and create new pathways in the client's brain. It is not the words that the coach says that count.

They are just the vehicle for the emotional loading. It is out of the emotional energy, generated by the coach's emotions resonating via the amygdala with the client's brain, that new associative pathways are built. In other words, it is the emotional timbre transmitted by the coach that resonates with the client's brain facilitating change or blocking it. In this way it is clear that executive coaching is a special and privileged form of attachment.

Attachment theory in use

You will remember that, in Chapter 2, we took some 1958 writing from Harlow about love, and substituted 'executive coach' for 'psychologist'. In what follows, keep substituting 'executive coach', or even 'me', for 'parent': and 'client' for 'child'.

Secure attachment
There are three main attachment categories between children and parents (Ruth Newton, 2008). The first category is to do with how securely-parented children become who they do. Ruth Newton describes how such children have their needs understood and appropriately met and so have a greater ability to explore the world and to do that with confidence knowing there are support systems in their parents when needed. They can influence others effectively in getting their own needs met through negotiating well in relationships that have reciprocity in them. They can understand others' positions and are socially competent. They regulate their emotions appropriately and can recover balance well from strong emotional experiences. And they have an inner sense of adequacy that shows itself outwardly in overall capability and competence.

Insecure – avoidant attachment
Contrast this with the second category of insecure-avoidant and ambivalent children. Such children are created by rejecting or inconsistent parents. They subsequently develop defensive strategies for dealing with their world, uncertain from a young age whether, if they reach out, their needs will be met or not. They are fundamentally afraid, though may have all kinds of strategies to hide that fact. They cannot regulate their emotions well, either ruminating or exploding, and they have a constant nagging doubt that they will be successful in getting what they want.
    Think Jim, having read that.

Insecure – disorganized attachment
Then there is a third category, to do with what children acquire from disorganized and chaotic parenting. They are fundamentally not just fearful inside but

terrified and frozen, and as a result as adults they will resort to all kinds of supportive dependent strategies to calm their inner lives. Alcohol intake and designer drugs do this well – they are adaptive in the short run but seriously maladaptive in the longer run. Alcohol and drug abuse are extremely good examples of adaptive templates that are maladaptive too.

New clients

The fact of the matter is that, when you meet a new coaching client, you have absolutely no idea what emotional structure forms the background to the exterior that your client presents to you and within the company. But you can be certain it is going to be from somewhere within the spectrum of the way early attachment happened – complicated by understanding too that these are not hard-and-fast categories. A child growing up might have had more of one and less of another, or none of one and lots of the other. The resilience of the human spirit makes what it can out of the circumstances of life. A tree that grows against all adversity on a windswept hillside may have, in its contortions, a beauty that is quite unlike how it would have looked grown in the shelter of an arboretum or self-seeded on a sunny hillside amongst many of its own kind. So it is with people. Learning to read the way emotions and experience have combined to make meaning for the person you coach, and so make the person who she or he is, is a special skill in a brain-based coach.

Back to the key question. What do I have to *do*?

Changing the Self

Here is what to do, keeping all the above in mind. Remind yourself that what you want to see change is the Self of the person you coach.

Only that? Yes, only that. Many coaches have been taught to stay away from something so central to the person as 'the Self'. But the new understandings that come from applied neuroscience make it quite clear that without engaging the Self of your client you cannot create change as the Self is the agent of change within your client's system.

But doing that requires you to have some sense of how the Self is constructed and works. The neurobiology of the Self is just beginning to be apparent, but if you start being aware of it in the following way you will not go far wrong.

The Self

First of all, there is a sense within the Self of the person who *knows* and the person who is known – sometimes called 'I' and 'me'. The capacity of the Self to regulate itself through the emotions gives us a clue as to what it is really about. It oversees the whole of the system that makes 'a person'.

Try this for a working metaphor.

Imagine the biggest collection of digital discs that you can – DVDs and CDs of a huge variety – stacked in a pile. Take them all away except the one right at the bottom of the pile. That is your Self as the baby that came into the world. The full stack of discs is your Self now.

Some of the discs were given to you, some you found for yourself. Some you know are ones that other people have – even though yours have special variations as do theirs. Some you can't recall acquiring or why you have them, and some you feel you have long outgrown. What you have is a stack of discs in parallel one to another that define you, sitting there. That is essentially what the brain has: a huge collection of parallel systems full of vast quantities of a wide variety of information. The question is, how does the individual access them?

If we really were talking just about discs, the answer would be 'one at a time'. But the brain has the ability to manage a huge number of parallel systems and combine them in a continuously dynamic way.

Self as central integrator

So think of the central hole down the stack of discs. Imagine that, from the earliest moment of life when you have come into the world, new experience not only creates new discs that start the stack growing but at the same time a special mechanism grows within the central core that is itself the central integrator of all the information on the discs, accessing the information in familiar ways and presenting it to the world. In this way both 'I' and 'others' know 'me'.

In relatively recent times, powerful search engines have made accessing huge amounts of computer information more and more productive. Relational databases create accessible and coherent meaning in data that would otherwise exist in an unusable jumble. So it is with the brain though very much more elegantly. What the Self does is to organize all the accumulated experience in increasingly familiar ways and begin to sort the sensory data coming in into familiar patterns. So the Self, as it is itself being constructed, also contributes to its own development. Bit by bit, out of the accumulated experience, emotion and meaning that is contained upon the discs, a stable and familiar Self begins to appear that is at the core of the person as the central integrator of the whole system that is 'mySelf'.

The Self is a very practised part of your client. It has grown over all the years of your client's life and it has been the means by which your client has established their own conscious understanding of themselves. It has also been the means by which your client has made sense to other people of who he or she is. It is not surprising then that, to your client, this remarkable Self is very precious, is to be guarded, is entirely taken for granted, is very tough, and can also be very vulnerable.

Relationships that change

Because the Self is constructed, as attachment theory shows us, out of the dynamic of relationships, the Self is always peculiarly susceptible to the effects of relationship. Think of falling in love. One of the consequences of falling in love is that the biochemical storm going through the brain at such a time creates a loss of a sense of Self. The detail of the experience might be quite different for a man and a woman, just as its physical consequences will be, but the process for the Self is exactly the same. Each wants to lose themself in the other person. That can get expressed physically or in a huge variety of different ways. But the essence of the disturbance of falling in love is that the boundaries of the Self become both much more sharply-defined – hence the intensity of touch – and at the same time much more fluid with regard to the other loved person. The urge is to have one's own Self submerged in the other person's.

Or think of a coaching client suddenly finding tears welling in their eyes. It happens with both men and women in coaching. What, as a coach, do you do? The social response is varied. Ignore it? Respond to the client's insistence to take no notice? Proffer a handkerchief? Reach for the tissue box? Break the session for five minutes?

As a brain-based coach, what you would know is that suddenly the Self has become peculiarly open to change. What the brain is doing through the body is communicating in the only way it can through the language of the body. So what the tears are saying is: 'Here I am releasing fluid to let you know my Self, my inner core, is feeling very fluid at the moment'. As with blushing, the body uses its own mechanisms to convey states that would otherwise not be apparent on the surface.

As a coach, what you would do would be to make a decision, in that moment, as to whether you help the Self settle back into its familiar shape or whether you use the fluidity that is there to fix some aspect of the new shape that is the purpose of the coaching. If you are a parent you will have done that spontaneously with a child who has been hurt or frightened and cried as you have managed the hurt, mopped the tears, and helped the child see the best way of dealing with such an event in the future. In coaching, done in the instant and done well, it is a very powerful way of effecting change and development. Done clumsily it leaves the person who was tearful only more certain that there is no help to be had and that all they can do is revert to the way they have always been.

Or think of another client who is having the demand for being different forced upon him by some organizational process or other. Edward, in Chapter 5, found himself in that situation. He had an acute sense of his Self being threatened by the demands being made on him. Though he could accept they made sense intellectually, in practice, in his situation, they made no sense at all.

His Self had been formed in very constrained circumstances but had served him well until the interpersonal world of his bit of the organization changed substantially without any prior warning. Like so many organizations it set out to do things that others were not expecting at all and that might have made perfectly good organizational sense from a design and development point of view but very poor interpersonal sense from a practical point of view.

Now we have all the building blocks in place for making sustainable change during coaching. The structure of the basic emotions is known, as is the way they are managed by the amygdala in the creating of meaning. The coaching relationship is the key variable in creating the conditions under which change may happen and development be facilitated. But that can only happen with prior background knowledge of how any particular brain was shaped in the circumstances of its own development. And you will know that however enjoyable your working relationship with your client is, or looks like it might be, your interest is not the relationship itself, which is only a carrier mechanism, but in effecting change in the templates of the brain. Your client's Self is in charge of it all, just as your Self is in charge of you. As a brain-based coach you have chosen to put your Self at the service of your client which is why you are both there. Your client wants to find out what your Self can do for the Self that has come for the coaching session.

A process

With all the elements and prior conditions in place, we are now ready to describe the process of what to actually do.

Simulation – the beginnings of modelling

The coaching encounters are structured around the coach's intention to create the beginnings of structural change so that the client can begin to model that change in the context of the coaching relationship. This is the absolute essence of Neurobehavioural Modelling. The coaching session will explore, in any appropriate way, not only what the client wants to accomplish but how to accomplish it and especially how to simulate it in the coaching session.

Simulation can happen in a variety of ways. Different coaches tend to have personal preferences depending, in part, on what they themselves have been trained in, have experienced, on their own temperament and style, and also on what they consider might best fit for the client as well as what the client says would be preferable. So, for instance, some coaches like role play exercises, others like triggering imaginal rehearsal, others like to create a plan of activity linked to goals, while still others use the empty-chair gestalt technique to generate the emotional arousal of what has been called projective identification.

We suggest you try silence as the way into imaginal rehearsal, using that remarkable route of a gaze quietly held to create the generative awareness that Nancy Kline (2009) has described in *More Time to Think*. Such a silence lets the amygdala settle down to as much of a resting a state as they ever allow for themselves and then opens up the actively resting mind to what Dan Siegel calls 'the plane of possibility'. Of course such a silence needs a focus, so before generative silence is encouraged to happen you will have worked out with your client what the focus of the imaginal process is going to be in that silence. And you will have given your client as much permission as necessary to interrupt the silence when there is something to be said that has been thought or felt. What the client is going to be doing is start to discover where attention should be focused within the goals you have agreed. What you the coach are doing is tuning your own brain so attentively that it keeps the other brain tuned into that state of generative awareness for achieving maximum effect.

Edward wanted to find out how to adapt to the firm's demands that he work more collaboratively with people. He was not against it in principle. But he simply felt he did not know how it looked or felt. In the collaborative process he wanted to find out how to manage the interpersonally competitive ways that men use to test hierarchy between them. It had not occurred to him that silence might help so the first stage was to let him experience silence, with the only goal being to let him find out what happens in the silence.

What he found out was that his mind kept flicking on to another project that was causing him quite a lot of stress. He could not focus in the silence, he said, because of the intrusiveness of the other thoughts – though he had never thought of things to do with work as being intrusive before. He thought the brain should be being busy like that, all the time.

So he agreed with his coach to shift the goal slightly and the task became to see if he could pick up on an awareness of the energy in his brain and redirect that energy. He decided that he would focus on a plan that had been in the back of his mind, to arrange a surprise visit to Vienna for an opera that he knew his girlfriend would love to go to.

To his surprise he found that difficult too, despite his intention to do it. The intrusive thoughts about the stressful project kept flicking in and he found he was spending the time trying to squash them and make space for the opera trip thoughts. But then he suddenly realized that that was where the energy was going. He was playing a kind of ping-pong with his thoughts. It felt like they were more in charge of him than he of them and he began to understand from within himself how anxiety, being related to fear and in consequence a survival emotion, could override his conscious wish to focus on something apparently more enjoyable.

So he asked what he should do. The coach said: 'How interesting it is that the problem that we have agreed would be good to sort out is about how to get into co-operative and collaborative relationships with your colleagues, and here you are having difficulty settling into a co-operative and collaborative relationship with your own brain. So let me ask you a question about you and your girlfriend. How do you make decisions together?'

'Oh, that's easy', said Edward. 'When there's anything important she asks me what I think. Then she always says that's a good idea and either she'll agree or she'll say something like "Well, I've been wondering about . . ." whatever it is. In fact she will have a whole plan worked out with very good thoughts in place. And I will typically say: "That's fine. Let's do that". And so she is happy and I'm happy if she's happy. That's how we sort out things together. Now I come to think about it that's how we sort out even simple things like shall we go out for dinner or which restaurant shall we go to. She factors in what I have said somehow and finds good answers. It works very well.'

'And you rely on her decisions almost completely, then, do you?' said the coach.

'Absolutely', said Edward. 'It really works.'

'Right now though,' said the coach, 'it's only you who can make the choice about how your brain is going to tackle the question of whether you focus on the thing that is worrying you or on the surprise opera trip. How are you going to go about that?'

Edward thought for a while. And then he said: 'What I usually say to my girlfriend is that I will do what she wants to do. So really I kind of give over my brain to her, don't I? I don't make independent decisions in that relationship. So what's happening in my brain in the silence we've been trying out is that my brain takes over because it's not used to being directed by me. What I've got to learn to do is use its energy to get it to do what I want it to do if I want it to do something other than it seems to have been trained to do.'

That seemed to the coach a pretty good formulation. 'Fantastic', he said. 'That sounds like a good mind at work to me. The trouble is what happens at work is changing.'

'Yes', said Edward. 'Well, what I am trying to do with my girlfriend is surprise her. My brain's not very used to that thought, it seems. And truth to say I'm a bit anxious about doing it anyway. But I do want to. What could I do to get my brain doing what I want it to?'

The coach stayed fixed on the coaching task of collaborative relationships. 'What would you do', he said, 'if you wanted some people to come to a dinner party?'

'Invite them, of course', said the client?

'What happens then', said the coach.

'All being well, they come', said the client.

'And what have they done to get there?' said the coach.

The client thought for a while, and then smiled quietly and said: 'Used some energy'.

'Very good', said the coach. 'What was it that got them using that energy in the way you wanted them to?'

'An invitation', said the client. 'You are a cunning bastard, you know. That's what I've got to do with my brain. Give it an invitation that, if it's good enough, will direct its energy in the way I want it to go. Is that what you are after?'

'If that's what you are after' said the coach. 'Let's try it, just in case you're right.'

And so they went back into generative silence, and after ten minutes the client said: 'I asked my brain if it would like to sort out the opera thing with me. It said it would. I've got the detail of the opera thing all worked out now. It's going to be a bigger surprise for her than I had first thought and I can see how it's all going to come together. Good. Let's get on with the collaborative stuff in the firm now.'

'Oh, we've done that already', said the coach. 'Give me a call when you have tried out whatever you are going to do.'

It was an interesting decision for the coach at that juncture whether he should have settled down with the client and done some specific imaginal rehearsal about how to engage in collaborative relationships within the firm; or whether he should risk the process generalizing itself to the client finding a way of inviting others into a collaborative relationship, using the discoveries he had made through the technique he had just been practising.

On balance the coach took the view that the experience the client had had was sufficiently strong and imbued with meaning for it to carry over into a real life situation. And he wanted to find out if that judgement was true, knowing they could always revert to imaginal rehearsal or some other kind of intervention at the next session if it proved not to be so. He knew also that Edward, being the conscientious person he was, would take what had happened away with him to use to the best of his ability. And the more he made the shift into real life situations on his own the stronger would be the new circuitry he established.

The essence of this whole sequence is that the coach arrived with Edward at a working solution (the invitation) that was already within Edward's experience. In consequence, the energy that had previously been used in anxiety could be channelled into already-existing networks, which is an infinitely easier process than trying to carve new ones.

Practice instructions

And that is the essence of brain-based coaching. It relies entirely upon an appreciation of what the brain is doing. It is remarkably simple and can be summed up in three practice instructions:

- keep the knowledge structure in mind
- be brave
- aim for intelligent emotions.

The first of these is exemplified overtly in Edward's case described above. 'Be brave' and 'intelligent emotions' need expanding a little.

Be brave

The practice of brain-based coaching is so uncharted that you will be sailing into waters where it is easy to imagine, as did the old mariners, that monsters lurk within the depths that are at the edge of the known world of your comfort zone. We can reassure you that it is not so, though only experience can make that certain for you.

So beginning to practice your coaching with the templates of the workings of the brain in mind needs a personal act of bravery that will also need to be repeated on a surprising number of occasions. Little things, like saying 'I don't know' to a client asking you something about the brain to which you had given no thought and have no knowledge, come into the brave category. And that is the way you will go on provoking your own learning and clients will learn from your fearlessness.

Intelligent emotions

Aiming for intelligent emotions is something we are ourselves still formalizing in our thoughts, but it seems important and this is where we have got to.

Daniel Goleman's 1997 formulation of *Emotional Intelligence* was an early statement at the very beginning of the modern neurosciences. It was one of those books that changes conversation radically. '**Emotional intelligence**' crops up in an extraordinary number of places.

We have been worried by the fact that, the way it seems to have developed, there is an overriding notion of 'quantity' about it, as with IQ. But a more fundamental concern we have is that it has a static quality about it as a concept – just as with IQ – whilst in fact it is intensely dynamic.

What we have wanted to focus on is not something to do with having or not having in a quantitative way, but on the dynamism of emotions put into use as the source of energy in the whole of the motivational system. Or, as we have expressed it earlier, e-motion. This shifts a working knowledge of the emotions into the focus that is necessary for a working coach. It is emotion(s) attached to experience that creates meaning. And the more current the emotion in relation to external reality the more likely that regulation will be possible; and then what is external will be perceived accurately and effectively.

There is a huge amount that could be said around that statement but this is not the time or place to state it even if we had finished formulating it to our own satisfaction. What we want to draw to your attention, as someone at the coalface of coaching, is that the concept of 'intelligent emotions' seems to generate a much higher level of easy acceptance among senior executives, who want to put it into use, than does the concept of 'emotional intelligence' – where the worry is about how much or little they might have. There is more about this in Chapter 9.

Summary

There is no escaping the fact that the client's brain is the organ upon which an effective coach is intending to leave a mark in order to create behavioural change that sticks. Your client's brain has its own purposeful integrity. The more you as a coach can understand that unique integrity the more the client will create a trusting relationship with you and engage actively in the processes of sustainable change and development. So this, we suggest, is how sustainable change can be created and takes place. Engage wholeheartedly with your own brain and the brain of your client. Use simulation, and then in real life situations, encourage practice, practice, practice. And that takes us back to Jim who becomes a main character again in Chapter 7.

7 Relationships that affect change and development

The person you coach almost certainly comes from a world in which hierarchy is deeply embedded in everyone's awareness: so deeply embedded that awareness of it is often well below the immediate threshold of consciousness a lot of the time. Yet its significance is operating continuously because the amygdala are scanning the whole time for the emotional significance of signals connected with hierarchy.

David Rock (2008) has developed a model of the-person-within-the-organization from a brain-based point of view. There are five elements to his model that goes by the mnemonic SCARF (Status, Certainty, Autonomy, Relatedness, Fairness). So S is for Status, and he suggests that where we stand in relation to others is of profound significance to the social brain.

Status

We focus more on the SCARF model in Chapter 9. But in the matter of organizational hierarchy status is an important component. Rock concentrates especially on the threat value connected with status. In a section headed 'Status and its Discontents' (2009) he writes:

> As humans, we are constantly assessing how social encounters either enhance or diminish our status. Research published by Hidehiko Takahashi *et al.* in 2009 shows that when people realize that they might compare unfavorably to someone else, the threat response kicks in, releasing cortisol and other stress-related hormones. (Cortisol is an accurate biological marker of the threat response; within the brain, feelings of low status provoke the kind of cortisol elevation associated with sleep deprivation and chronic anxiety.)
>
> Separately, researcher Michael Marmot, in his book *The Status Syndrome: How Social Standing Affects Our Health and Longevity* (Times

Books, 2004), has shown that high status correlates with human longevity and health, even when factors like income and education are controlled for. In short, we are biologically programmed to care about status because it favors our survival. . . . A study by Joan Chiao in 2003 found that the neural circuitry that assesses status is similar to that which processes numbers; the circuitry operates even when the stakes are meaningless, which is why winning a board game or being the first off the mark at a green light feels so satisfying. Competing against ourselves in games like solitaire triggers the same circuitry, which may help explain the phenomenal popularity of video games.

Understanding the role of status as a core concern can help leaders avoid organizational practices that stir counterproductive threat responses among employees. For example, performance reviews often provoke a threat response; people being reviewed feel that the exercise itself encroaches on their status. This makes 360-degree reviews, unless extremely participative and well-designed, ineffective at generating positive behavioral change. Another common status threat is the custom of offering feedback, a standard practice for both managers and coaches. The mere phrase 'Can I give you some advice?' puts people on the defensive because they perceive the person offering advice as claiming superiority. It is the cortisol equivalent of hearing footsteps in the dark.

Organizations often assume that the only way to raise an employee's status is to award a promotion. Yet status can also be enhanced in less-costly ways. For example, the perception of status increases when people are given praise. Experiments conducted by Keise Izuma in 2008 show that a programmed status-related stimulus, in the form of a computer saying 'good job', lights up the same reward regions of the brain as a financial windfall. The perception of status also increases when people master a new skill; paying employees more for the skills they have acquired, rather than for their seniority, is a status booster in itself.

Values have a strong impact on status. An organization that appears to value money and rank more than a basic sense of respect for all employees will stimulate threat responses among employees who aren't at the top of the heap. Similarly, organizations that try to pit people against one another on the theory that it will make them work harder reinforce the idea that there are only winners and losers, which undermines the standing of people below the top 10 percent.

Before picking up on this in more detail, let us link it to some recent research that neuroscientist Christof Koch reported in the journal *Nature* (January 2012). It takes us back to thinking about the Self. The Self is vitally connected to any perceptions that affect itSelf – a circularity that cannot be escaped and that is at the heart of everything about every one of us.

Connectomics

But before we get to Koch, '**connectomics**' is a recent aspect of the neurosciences that needs bringing on to stage. It has the capacity to take the research neurosciences in directions that would have seemed impossible only ten years ago and that mirror the interest coaches have in how things connect together in the brain of the client who is seeking change and development. It is such a new science that sometimes it is called '**connectonomics**'; but marketing companies who are interested in the neurosciences have rather taken over the use of that word so 'connectomics' seems to be winning out in the scientific community.

Earlier, it was described how the cognitive social neuroscientists and the interpersonal neurobiologists are taking slightly different tracks in their approaches to understanding the brain.

The first group are fascinated by localization and expect that, one day, the accumulation of thousands of bits of experimental information about which bit of the brain does what will make it possible to construct a working understanding of the brain. It is something of a jigsaw with thousands of neuroscientists bringing new bits of the jigsaw to the table and then finding that other neuroscientists can redefine the part that they have brought until eventually there is pretty solid agreement on the bits. There are now 60,000 neuroscientific papers being published each year – more than 5,000 every month – which is a lot of jigsaw pieces.

The interpersonal neurobiologists, on the other hand, have more of an interest in the person being presented by the brain. What they want to know is how the brain creates the person, and vice versa. It is an approach with which we have some natural sympathy. Helping this development is the new science of connectomics. It is setting out to describe the 'connectome', or the way the whole complex structure of the brain's neural circuits are interconnected and intercommunicate. Olaf Sporns coined the term 'connectomics' in 1995, and what is beginning to be shown is that there seem to be twelve key hubs on each side of the brain that have special power. In reporting the work of Sporns *et al.* (2005), Andy Coghlan (2011) observes:

> Not all brain regions are created equal – instead, a 'rich club' of 12 well-connected hubs orchestrates everything that goes on between your ears. . . . As part of an ongoing effort to map the human 'connectome' – the full network of connections in the brain – Martin van den Heuvel of the University Medical Center in Utrecht, the

Netherlands, and Olaf Sporns of Indiana University, Bloomington scanned the brains of 21 people as they rested for 30 minutes.

The researchers used a technique called **diffusion tensor imaging** to track the movements of water through 82 separate areas of the brain and their interconnecting neurons. They found 12 areas of the brain had significantly more connections than all the others, both to other regions and among themselves.

'These 12 regions have twice the connections of other brain regions, and they're more strongly connected to each other than to other regions,' says Van den Heuvel. 'If we wanted to look for consciousness in the brain, I would bet on it turning out to be this rich club,' he adds. . . .

'This network makes the way the brain functions more robust overall, but it could also leave the entire system vulnerable to breakdown if key hubs are damaged or disabled,' says Van den Heuvel.

After mapping the connections, Van den Heuvel's team manipulated the data to see what might happen if parts of the rich club were damaged. The simulated brain lost three times as much function if the elite hubs were taken out than if random parts of the brain were lost.

'If [one of these] regions goes down, it can take the others down too, just like when banks failed in the global economic crisis,' says Van den Heuvel.

Back to what Christof Koch reported in *Nature*. He writes:

Neuroscience: The connected self
We moderns believe that our momentary, subjective experience is intimately linked to events in the brain. One set of neurons fires, and we perceive an apple's colour, while a different population of cells gives rise to its taste. Yet the self is also stable: turn the brain off, as happens during heart surgery when the body is cooled to frigid temperatures, and on recovery, the patient's character, personality, habits and long-term memories remain intact. It is these stable aspects of the self, rather than the ebb and flow of our thoughts and percepts, that physicist-turned-neuroscientist Sebastian Seung seeks to explain in *Connectome*, published in early 2012.

Dynamic understanding

Putting the reports of Coghlan and Koch together, it is clear that the brain sciences are right at the beginning of starting to re-define the brain in terms of its wiring diagram – its circuits and connections – rather than simply its structure and the localization of function. That is to say, the science is moving from a static to a dynamic understanding of how the whole system works. Eventually the two will have to come together, but at the present state of affairs in the neurosciences the dynamic shift is fascinating and it is important to remark upon it for two reasons.

Implication for coaches

The first is that for you, as a coach interested in the brain sciences, it is crucial to realize just how much on the edge we are of continuous development in our understanding of the brain. The next twenty years looks like it will be explosive in the growth of knowledge and the understanding of how it all works. So the journey you have started, in reading this book thus far, is going to be an ongoing one. And the explosive growth has huge implications for our understanding of individuals and of how they give their best in organizations – the professional focus at the heart of executive coaching.

Implications for organizations

The second reason for introducing connectomics is to observe that the brain sciences are driving ahead in getting hold of, what in organizational terms, would be called 'management information'. Organizations, however, are not in parallel developing their capacity to image what is going on inside organizations.

So suddenly there is the beginnings of a real imbalance between what we are starting to know about people and about how organizations are falling behind in an understanding of their own human processes and the take-up of this knowledge. A new science of management information about people, the brain-based dynamics of the interactions between them and the impact of all that on performance, is hardly on the organizational agenda at all. As coaching clients come from this environment it is important to have this dilemma in mind, as there might be an awkward period of time, perhaps a decade or more, when working knowledge about people is well in advance of organizational capacity to use it. This has potential for discord. It is also a remarkable opportunity for the brain-based coaching community to have a signal effect upon the human relationship side of organizational life.

Hierarchy

A theorist whose thinking presaged some of these issues was Elliott Jaques (1997), the developer of stratified systems theory. Jaques was especially interested in the span of control that individuals have inside organizations and why hierarchies arise in consequence. Thirty years of observations, many at the Glacier Metal Company, led him to conclude that what distinguishes one hierarchical level from another is what he called 'the target completion time of the longest task, project or program assigned to that role'. For a machine operator the longest task might be the half hour it took to set up the machine, or the two hours it took to mill a piece of metal to its precise shape. It might be two years for an accountant to rebuild a complex reporting system that was being turned over to computerized systems whilst keeping the old one going at the same time. It might be five years for a CEO to turn around a failing company – the time that the Royal Bank of Scotland is expecting to take to return itself to profit from its disastrous acquisition strategy and the banking crisis of 1998.

Relationships

Despite being both a doctor and a practising psychoanalyst as well as a management theorist, Jaques did not turn his attention to the nature and quality of relationships inside organizations. It is our contention, however, that from the way the brain sciences are developing, whatever the span of control over their own or others' activities that people have inside organizations, the key element in their effectiveness (output/performance/deliverables) and the sustainability of that effectiveness will arise from the quality of relationship that exists within the system of which they are a part.

Brain sciences used to rely on post-mortem findings to understand how the living system might work. Organizations tend to rely on post-mortem – or at least *post-hoc* – data to get a fix on what the organization is up to. All reporting in organizations is essentially after-the-event. It describes what has happened, not what is actually happening or is likely to happen. Forecasting techniques are notoriously unreliable – which is surprising when human beings are intensely reliable and predictable (even reliably unreliable and unpredictable), once understood in their individuality. What makes so much forecasting unreliable is that the models used assume that individuals have common attributes. That leads to lowest common denominator high error outcomes. What the brain sciences are showing us is that individuals have common attributes that lead to *un*common outcomes because of the uniqueness of each individual's brain. Prediction needs to be able to factor in *dis*similarity, which is where brain-to-brain coaching starts from.

What a status-driven model of the organization requires is that the escape/avoidance emotions are kept in play. What a network-driven model of the organization requires is that the attachment emotions are kept in play. The first group of emotions keeps people where they are. The second group releases productive energy for pursuing the operational and strategic goals of the organization and not, primarily, the personal goals of survival. These are the same attachment emotions that are the key to the effectiveness of coaching using Neurobehavioural Modelling.

Attachment again

This brings the case study of Jim (Chapter 3, pp. 33–34) back into the picture via some ideas that were published by David Drake in 2009. Concerned with the development of leaders, Drake was interested in the benefits of finding a coherent narrative within the leaders he worked with as to how they might talk about and live their lives. What does the Self understand of itSelf, we might say? Attachment theory was his starting point.

The stories that executives tell about themselves during coaching sessions can be like a window on to the whole of their interior landscape. What you, the coach, need to be tuned into is the emotional patterning of the behaviours that underlie the events that you hear about. Secure leaders who can regulate their own emotions, and who have a coherent narrative of their lives, can (through resonance) regulate the emotional systems of those they lead. They are secure and pass that security on. This is true too in the coaching relationship.

Jim

Jim had completely blown his stack with Sally, his wife. In our earlier account he was in a coaching session evidencing all the signs of his HPA axis firing away, having no insight as to his part in what had happened, and at risk of being trapped into some highly unsatisfactory outcomes in both his marriage and his job. It was suggested that a way into the situation with someone like Jim would be to start from where his brain starts most easily: absorbing information that is new and, for him, lacking in emotional undertones. So we suggested the session might start by giving him some insight into the way his HPA axis had been churning all weekend and was still reverberating.

But if coaching is to shift Jim's behaviour *he* has to want to shift it, and he will only want that if he can experience options and outcomes himself by modelling them with you. A working choice as this session develops would be to get Jim to recreate and explore the strong feelings he has been having and imagine the possible outcomes at work and at home – in other words, where his feelings might lead him.

Many clients initially resist the idea that their feelings are leading them. It is not what the executive ethos preaches. They hang firmly on to knowing it is rationality, not irrationality in the Platonic/Descartesian dichotomous world we have created in the West, that defines our actions.

A way into that false dichotomy is to ask Jim what it was that directed his actions throughout the weekend. He will undoubtedly offer Sally's behaviour and his own tiredness as two good reasons from his point of view. But ask him gently, though insistently, what his part in it was. A pleasant weekend would have been much more refreshing – what stopped him from creating such a weekend? And if Sally is to blame again, ask him: 'Is that how he defines their relationship? Does his state depend entirely upon Sally?' If the answer is 'yes', then a good route to take is to ask whether Sally's state might also depend upon him. And if he says 'no', or not always, then push further into exploring how differences in experience are directly related to differences in the prevailing emotional state – that feelings drive perception which in turn drives behaviour to which feelings are linked which creates perception and so on and so on and so on. Perception driven by feelings is the key to behaving as we do and so the key to change.

Underpinning this dialogue will be the explicit understanding that, in any interpersonal situation where change is required, the only person any one person can change is themselves. By knowing the key role of perception (and hence the amygdala) in the key messages that are sent and the profound effect they have on other people (and their amygdala), and by knowing that the more attached one person is to another the more profoundly the effect is manifested, the mechanism that makes change possible begins to be within Jim's control.

The key relationship of interest here is Jim's relationship with his own Self. If that is the only place from which real and sustainable change can come, it is there that change has to happen first of all. Then there is some possibility of Jim learning that he can really be the modifier of what happens between himself and Sally – which is just one element in the change for which he has engaged in coaching.

In the earlier account of Jim's return from abroad and the weekend that followed, what happened and the way Jim treated Sally was described. In the actual coaching context this specific information would almost certainly not have been immediately available. It would simply be Jim at a coaching session and in the mood that he is in. How much would you, as his coach, be pushing to find out what really happened at the weekend? And would you press firmly enough for Jim to tell you what actually happened in the car on the way home from the airport? You know enough from Jim's history and why he has come into coaching to be able to be pretty certain that whatever did happen at the weekend (of which you are only seeing the residual misery) was an experience of the kind that is precipitating the organizational concerns. Is your own coaching attachment to Jim secure enough to take on the risk of walking into the marital tension territory?

It certainly is territory that can't be avoided for a brain-based coach. Jim's Self is looking for your expertise in understanding himSelf – what makes him tick – and how you are going to make things different with him. He is a continuous human being in which 'work' and 'home' are different places but not essentially different experiences, and certainly not managed by different Jims.

The stage changes, the characters change, but the plot stays essentially the same because the way his brain works stays essentially the same. His connectome is the way it is.

With your working knowledge of the emotional system, and the way escape/avoidance reactions are the default mechanism, and the state that Jim is in, you can be certain that there are perturbations in his system which, if you do not get them up into working consciousness, will leave Jim no better off for your session with him. He may of course feel that he has had a good session without your going anywhere near the detail of the weekend – knowing there is someone taking an interest in him gives him some courage for the day ahead, and he has had sufficient time in the privacy of the coaching session to de-stress a bit. But those are all incidental outcomes of any good social encounter. The focus of the coaching session is much more specific. It is to get his own awareness of the way his emotional system is driving him up into working consciousness so that he can make some effective decisions about what he wants to do about it. That is what the coaching relationship is for.

Jim's Chairman is focused on his *behaviours*. A coaching focus knows that behaviour is the outcome of thought and feelings, but that it is in the feeling system that the emotional drivers determine what Jim actually does. His thinking simply rationalizes it – as in blaming Sally, or justifying his behaviour to his boss by the results he gets. But these are not explanations for his state, although they will be given as such. They are simply his attempts to understand. Your special privilege as his coach is to get inside his head, look at the world through his eyes, and explore with him the circuits that are objectively no longer serving him well. Then you can offer him the opportunity to make a change.

Tailored sense-making

There is a long-standing belief coming out of the psychotherapy and counselling fields that the opportunity to talk about difficult emotional events will itself be beneficial. It is a generalization that is known to be too superficial to be relied upon and it is now understood that talking about feelings may simply rehearse and reinforce them. Even after major traumatic events, many individuals come out of the trauma best by being encouraged to deal with it in whatever way they have learnt to deal with adverse events in their lives. They make sense of it in their own terms. Human beings are intensely adaptable and, all brains being different, many brains will have developed their own templates for dealing with all kinds of situations even if those templates are not the ones that the unscientific solutions of twentieth-century psychotherapies said they should be.

But there *are* some external imperatives bearing down upon Jim from his organization and also upon you, his coach. In accepting the organization's brief what you, Jim's coach, know is that you cannot change or develop Jim but what you can do is create the conditions under which he *wants* to change and develop. Then you can guide that process.

It is almost certain that getting Jim to that critical point of really wanting to change will not be possible without using the whole of his experience to get his awareness to the point of realization that there are completely understandable irrationalities going on within him. If, like many executives, he is stuck in a highly-developed belief that it *is* the rational, thinking side of him that is in control, then using the idea of a rational (thinking) and irrational (emotional) side to him may be a compromise you have to make *as long as* you hang on hard to the idea that what we have chosen to call irrational does in fact obey the laws of its own logic. All the laws of the emotional system are designed to both protect the individual and make attachments as secure as possible. This is a complicated double demand that often results in contradictory messages, like Jim swearing viciously at someone he also says he loves and would hate to lose, or annihilating a subordinate he knows is of great value to the company.

It is not about looking for 'an explanation' as to why Jim does this, for the explanation is entirely coherent within the design of the brain. Jim does this because that is how his brain functions, and it learnt to function that way because at some critical period of his development it learnt to function that way. The specifics of that patterning could be determined by detailed enquiry, perhaps. But they are not in any way crucial to the possibility of change. What is crucial to the possibility of change is Jim's real appreciation that the emotional patterns – templates – that you are helping him bring into his immediate conscious awareness do underpin his behaviour and can, if he chooses, be changed.

Back to the King's Cross underground metaphor. What line does Jim want to be on – the one that's familiar, but is taking him to destinations that are doing him no good and forcing others into places where they have no wish to be? Or the one that is new and is taking him to a different place? That is the essence of the choices being exposed to him. In his coaching session he can model those options and, if he wants to try a new line, start testing out what that would feel like and what the behavioural consequences would be. Back at Chapter 5 (pp. 57–58) Maggie's client arrived at that point when a mix of coaching and a daughter's challenge focused his awareness on the choices that he had and the behavioural consequences arising from them. Jim has not got there yet. He is stuck in a redundant pattern of earlier success which will limit his future success and his enjoyment unless change can come about.

Five strategies

The five narrative strategies that Drake says he finds helpful in coaching contain four that we have independently also been building into this process and that, like Drake's, come from attachment theory. The first is providing clients with coaching sessions that have a real sense of being a safe haven. Not just a haven, though, but a place where the brain can buzz productively in its own interest. Under such conditions the amygdala are as much at rest as they ever are and so open up the emotional highways to the possibility of new tracks being taken, which is the basis of change. Having the skill of creating generative attention is very useful here.

The second of Drake's strategies is about using rapport – what we have referred to with Jim as gentle insistence. It is an aspect of the coaching encounter that both relies upon trust and also generates trust when well done because the client has the sense that you know where you are going in the labyrinths of the mind and that you hold the keys to discovery. You do, by unlocking the capacities of your client's brain to function at its best.

The third is to encourage the coach to use the coaching sessions as what Drake calls 'a laboratory for the study of clients' attachment-related behaviours'. More specifically, we suggest, holding a working model of the emotions in mind is like having a road map in front of you and guiding the discovery of what you want your client to know. The coaching session will contain discoveries that could not have been known about in advance. Think of your coaching more as opening a new novel than entering a laboratory. The discoveries will be about the plot of the person's life based upon its unique emotional structure linked to the experiences to which those emotions are attached. For your client this is not an experiment, it is life.

Drakes' fourth rubric for coaching from an attachment perspective is to link current behaviours with discoveries about childhood patterns. We agree, though again stress that the main purpose of those discoveries is not for the sake of discovery *per se* but to so engage your client with an understanding of how his or her brain works that there is huge engagement in the excitement of creating changes in it. Once that has been accomplished, your client's brain will do an enormous amount of the work that would otherwise be hard won if won at all.

And fifth, Drake encourages coaches to model what being an effective listener and caregiver is like, with the expectation that your clients will thereby extend their own range of facilitation skills. Our own fascination with coaching is to honour and value the uniqueness of the individual who comes into coaching. Coaching from a brain-based point of view is for the purposes of creating the conditions under which development can take place. If your client takes away something of your style too then that may be a bonus for you both, but that is not what coaching from a brain-based perspective is essentially about. It is for your client to know more about, trust and be fascinated by their own brain and the way it always works productively even if context makes it seem unproductive: and then to know that to let the brain do well what it can do very well, which is to make the adaptations that are needed. It is to that end that the next chapter focuses especially on affective interaction.

Summary

In working as a coach who uses the brain sciences as the basis for understanding your client, there is no escaping the fact that the brain sciences themselves are at an early stage of development. A great deal of information comes from the laboratories that are trying to piece together the functioning of the brain on the giant jigsaw principle. But other laboratories are more interested in how the whole connects together and what influence each part has upon the others. The jigsaw approach feels relatively static, while connectivity is more dynamic and is the way the brain organizes itself. In coaching, the key to using knowledge about the brain effectively is to learn to value the uniqueness of each client through building up an understanding of the way emotional patterning influences all your client's actions: and using the energy of that process to create a change in your client's capacity to know and trust their own brain.

8   Affective interaction

'Affect' is the word traditionally used in psychology and psychiatry to mean 'things to do with emotions and feelings that show outwardly what might be going on inwardly'. It is a useful word, even if not specific in terms of the feelings/emotions distinction that we think of such importance. There are occasions where there is no particular need to distinguish between feelings and emotions. That is when 'affect' is a good word to have to hand.

Decisions, decisions

In his 2009 book *How We Decide*, Jonah Lehrer recounts the circumstances of how, in the first Gulf War in 1991, Lieutenant Commander Michael Riley, on the destroyer *HMS Gloucester*, fatigued by long hours on duty in the cramped radar scanning room of his ship, made a vital decision about something that only appeared as one blip among many on his radar screen. He had no means of knowing with any kind of certainty whether what he saw might be a friendly American plane or an enemy missile that could cause colossal damage to the battleship *USS Missouri* at which it was aimed. With absolutely no basis for a rational decision he had whatever the blip was on his screen shot out of the sky. Four hours later it was confirmed that his instinctive reaction had been right. To his immense relief he had not just killed two American aircrew, but had shot down a missile with the power to sink the *Missouri*.

In subsequent detailed trawling of the vast amount of electronically-recorded data surrounding the incident no rational basis for the decision could be found and yet it had been absolutely right.

In game theory the odds of two pilots killed against the possibility of a battleship being sunk would have justified the decision to shoot; though had it been two pilots killed from friendly fire the odds would have looked different *post hoc* than in the heat of the decision process. This kind of zero sum game assessment, so beloved of risk strategists, was not anywhere in the lieutenant commander's mind. He did not know what the basis of his decision was. All he knew was that there was something wrong with that blip.

Lehrer records how a neuroscientist called Gary Klein became intrigued by what had happened and by the complete lack of explanation for why the right decision had been made. Why had *that* blip on the radar screen, among all that he had monitored, troubled the lieutenant commander? Long-fascinated by the decision-making process, Klein set out to find why.

After repeatedly going over the records of the visual data that Riley had been scanning Klein discovered that the blip in question had not appeared on the array until eight seconds after it would have been normal for an American plane to appear. That eight seconds meant that the blip came after the third sweep of the radar scanner, when normally a plane would have been picked up on its first sweep. That difference meant that the blip causing Riley so much concern was travelling at a lower altitude than a plane should be travelling. It was flying at one thousand feet – the height of a missile – instead of the three thousand feet that was the corridor for a returning aircraft.

None of these facts were in either Riley's consciousness or available from the huge amounts of data captured and supposedly integrated by the electronic surveillance systems. What his brain was telling him was that whatever it was it was rogue, and what his training told him was that, if rogue, take action. Which he did. That is affective interaction at work within the brain of a single individual – his own interaction within the unknown yet integrated complexities of his own brain's systems.

Research studies by Walter Mischel and colleagues (1972) with children at Stanford in the early 1970s have recently attracted a lot of renewed attention. They show affective interaction at an early stage of development having profound consequences in life. Known as the Marshmallow experiments and variously repeated in modern times, they focus on a particular aspect of the brain functioning within the individual and the implications of that for social effectiveness.

Mischel took pre-school children, one at a time, into an experimental room where there was a chair and a table. On the table was a small treat that had previously been established as the child's favourite – a marshmallow, a pretzel stick, or an Oreo cookie. The experimenter explained that the treat was there for the child to eat, that the experimenter was going to leave the child in the room for a short while, and if the child could delay eating the treat until the experimenter returned then there would be two treats instead of just the one and they could be eaten straight away. Mischel conceived this experiment as an enquiry into delayed gratification. Would the child hold out for a larger reward or yield to the immediate opportunity to have the treat?

Children were left alone for fifteen minutes – a huge amount of time for a young child. It was observed that the children who tried to delay eating the treat adopted a wide range of tactics to prevent themselves from taking it. Some sat very quietly, others turned their backs, others hid under the table, one child took the cookie apart, licked off the cream on the inner surfaces, and then put the cookie back together trying to make it look as if it had not been tampered with. Other children ate the treat within thirty seconds. Mischel showed that the capacity in pre-school children to delay gratification was widely variable.

Modern interest in these experiments comes from Mischel's later involvement with his experimental subjects. They had all been children at Stanford University's Big Nursery School, also attended by Mischel's daughters and where some, in the course of time, became part of his daughters' networks of friends. During everyday family life Mischel began to hear about various children's accomplishments and foibles and thought it might be worth looking at a longitudinal study related to his earlier findings. What had happened developmentally to his delayed and immediate gratifiers?

More than ten years after the original experiment Mischel discovered that children who had delayed gratification were described by their parents as being significantly more competent socially and academically than those children who had gone for immediate gratification. In further follow-up, more than twenty-five years after the original experiment, Mischel showed that the capacity, aged 4, to delay gratification correlated significantly with SATS scores. Delayers got higher SATS scores by a substantial margin. A 2011 report (Casey *et al.*, 2011), nearly forty years on, showed that the differences – as expressed in higher economic and social success – continued throughout adult life. Brain imaging results in the adults who had been the original experimental subjects showed different brain mass in the prefrontal cortex, which is concerned with decision-making, and in the **ventral striatum**, which is concerned with pleasure, reward and addiction. Recent, related experiments are suggesting that it may be possible to find markers in childhood brain development that are predictors of life success.

Whilst Mischel's experiments are described in terms of psychosocial theory linked to brain structure, Lehrer's account of Riley's actions on *HMS Gloucester* takes a biochemical rather than a brain mass vantage point. He describes how dopamine (see Chapter 3) is the specific facilitator of decision-making behaviours because it has the capacity to trigger reward/no reward circuits and so create 'go' or 'no go' (prediction-error) signals. When something that had previously appeared fine appeared infinitesimally less than fine the brain was surprised and so set out to reassess its own predicting mechanism. Specialized brain cells (**spindle cells**, so-called because they do not branch at the axonal point in the way that other neurons do) get dopamine flooding through the brain at speed. Not surprisingly, particular areas of the brain are implicated in these processes too. You will experience these fine dopamine balances when you yourself have half seen something that you know you ought to react to but do not and then later on say to yourself or someone else: 'I knew that but . . .', or 'If only . . .'.

Neurochemistry of decision-making

With the later advantage of the modern neurosciences the Marshmallow experiments suggest that the neurochemistry of decision-making is established from an early age. That would not surprise a brain-based coach, as it fits well with the developing understanding of how early patterns resonate through life. And it is in these early patterns that the neurobiology of individual behaviour becomes defined.

Affective interaction

What about the interaction *between* systems – you and your client? Brain to brain, amygdala to amygdala, limbic system to limbic system, there is a colossal capacity for one person's emotional system – that person's neurochemistry – to resonate with and regulate the system of another or the systems of many others. It is entirely what social interaction and effective leadership rely upon. Dan Siegel has neatly called this 'The Neurobiology of "We" '. How do relationships, mind and brain interact to shape who we are and what we do?

As a coach it is possible to continuously watch the ebb and flow of what is happening to and in a client whilst also tuning your own capacity to be both observer of your own and your client's state, and a person who can formulate what is happening in terms of the brain information and models that you have inside your head.

Affect

So in this affective 'ballet' that, as human beings, we are each part of when we interact with any other person, what drives the affect? How as a coach should you think about and understand it? And how can you turn that information and understanding to good account?

Emotions are the irreducible feelings. Emotions control and manage energy flow. A client brings a mind to you and you have the opportunity and responsibility to tune your mind for the benefit of that client's mind. It is a process called resonating. It both catches and creates the emotional state – the affective state – of the client with whose affect you are engaged.

A client struggling with the aftermath of the latest row with her boss brings that row to you in the shape of the effect that her boss has had upon her affect. She might sit tense, or sad, or slumped, or feistily in front of you – or even oscillating between all those states and more – as her feelings flood the whole of her nervous system and convey their messages to you in every fibre of her being.

Dan Siegel considers that emotion is an inner state and feelings are what we observe within ourselves. For him, affect is the outward appearance of the inner state combined with the feelings that we experience happening. He observes that scientists have not yet properly cracked the problem or shared common understanding about what emotions really are. Our best working guess, at this stage of knowledge, and inspired by Dan Siegel's thinking, is that indeed the emotions are the source of energy and, being part of the tripartite structure of the mind, the key source of energy that transmutes relationship into action that makes it possible to make the best possible sense of information of all kinds.

At the Annual Conference of the NeuroLeadership Institute in Los Angeles in 2009 Dan Siegel gave a graphic demonstration of how the brain works to create the way the mind displays itself. From notes and recollection, this is how it went.

Differentiation and integration

'Who here sings in a choir?' Dan asked the audience of some two hundred coaches and neuroscientists. About a dozen hands went up. 'Fine', he said, 'you are probably quite used to performing in public. Might I invite you all to come up here and I will show you how the mind works.' With some slightly nervous laughter from the hand-raisers and a good deal of amusement from the rest, the volunteers found themselves on the platform facing the audience.

'We've got all these helpful people here on the stage', said Dan. 'They are all the same because they are human beings but they are all different and it's the differences we see most clearly. Our brains are wired to search for differences first. So think of them as being differentiated. That's exactly the same for your brain. It is a mass of parts that look pretty much the same but are in fact highly differentiated. Let's get this brain working. What I want each member of this choir to do first of all is to sing a single note together and hold it. Would one of you pitch a single note, please? Then when I raise my hand to start, will you all sing that same note and hold it.'

Being willing participants, it happened easily. The audience heard a single note that had a bit of variation in its volume as people stopped to catch breath. But after the first slight anticipatory surprise of briefly waiting for and then hearing the sound emerge, the experience quickly became boring. Dan waved his hands and stopped the sound.

'Thank you', he said again. 'Now I want each member of the choir to think of a song. When I raise my hand to start, I want each person in the choir to cover their ears to drown out all other sounds and sing their own song.'

What the audience heard of course was the most dreadful cacophony. Each part was functioning perfectly well and some parts looked as if they might even be enjoying themselves. But the total result was a dense jungle of sound in which no tune could be discerned. No specific memory for any detail could be established, just the undifferentiated sense of an overall cacophony.

'Okay okay', said Dan, bringing the singing to a halt. 'The point has been made. There is no harmony of any kind is there? But they were all performing perfectly well individually. What I want the choir to do now is get together and agree upon a song they all know and would like to sing for you.' So the choir did this and the audience heard 'Amazing Grace' in a completely unrehearsed rendition. The audience had an experience of highly differentiated beings acting willingly in a unitary fashion all taking account of each other and contributing their own efforts to the total outcome. What a wonderful demonstration not only, by analogy, of a brain in action but a team or a whole organization.

Three different states

Rigidity

As the members of the choir resumed their seats, Siegel said: 'What you have just been observing is the three different states of the energy processes within the brain that create how the mind works. The first, represented by the single monotonous note, was rigidity. Everyone was making the same sound and so they were all linked together, but it was at the price of anything that we might call effective complexity. We had linkage without **differentiation** so there was no place for integration. The differences between differentiated parts were completely obscured in one single system. It sounded as if something had got stuck and in no time you were bored and restless. It is not something you would willingly choose to listen to for long, I guess. Rigidity is a state that hinders the processing of information because it has only one task which is to stay as it is.'

Chaos

'The second demonstration of everyone singing their own song produced chaos – there was nothing coherent in it at all. The individual parts, if you could have heard any of them, were each coherent but there was nothing happening that was cohesive. That's a very important distinction when thinking about integrated systems. The bits can be working fine and individually coherent. But they are not cohesive unless they are working together. That's what the members of poorly attached families are like.'

Harmony/integration

'But finally you heard something that was harmonious. All the differentiated parts were processing the same information, though no-one had told them in detail what it was but they each had much the same data inside them and they were able to listen to and for each other and modulate – regulate – what they were doing in relation to each other. They were resonating together. So that's the brain and its differentiated systems. When the differentiated parts are working well together the plane of possibility opens up. That choir would have tried anything we had asked of them.' It is not difficult to imagine the fascination of the audience witnessing such a live and intensely productive metaphor.

In Chapter 5 (pp. 57–58) there was an account of how Maggie, a coach, observed a difference in the physical posture of her client and then found in the session that followed that the observation – which had caused a blip of surprise in her when she saw it – presaged an extraordinary shift in her client. The groundwork in coaching, and a chance remark from within an intensely valued relationship with his daughter, had given the client an insight into his behavioural options that had not thus far been available to him. He had moved from his previous rigidity ('Well, I am who I am and I haven't done too badly so far') to the flexibility of being willing to engage in relationships much more productively at work. In the dynamic interaction of information, energy and relationship an accumulation of information (about how the brain works from his coach) has been triggered (by a relationship with his daughter) into a different focus for the energy of his emotions to flow back into relationship (with his staff). Harmony was within sight. His coach had seen it in his body and his staff would see it in his style. More especially his daughter would see more of it in the Dad she loved and who loved her.

The single note that started the choir demonstration is a good analogy for the internal state that we described in relation to Edward when he first came for coaching. Family life during his childhood had little emotional tone in it and he developed patterns that were fine for the pursuit and application of technical knowledge but lacking in emotional resonance of any breadth – an existence that might fairly be described musically as being within a narrow range. Under organizational stress his inner, early-morning-waking world tried out rigid, simplistic, undeveloped, single-issue, one-off solutions – create a winning row, invoke employment law, abandon the meetings – any of which would have done him damage and all of which also showed how little interpersonal skill he had at this organizational level. With his girlfriend he rode pillion on her emotional power. The coach's task was to offer Edward the chance to start tuning the instrument of himself differently.

Elizabeth

The chaos of the cacophony – everyone making their own music but having nothing linking them together – is the state in which Elizabeth came to coaching. She had come as something of an emergency. Her boss was insisting that she take a week off work because of her behaviour. He wanted her to attend a medical appointment, and had expressed serious concern for her well-being. Elizabeth was insistent she was fine, did not want to do either of those things, but did agree to see a coach.

Elizabeth was the senior project manager in a complex IT infrastructure redevelopment programme within a major government department. It was known to be going badly wrong. It had been established as a three-year programme for integrating the IT systems that managed materiel supply for all the armed services. All the systems had grown up haphazardly on many sites across the country when materiel was looked after by the three services independently. They were never designed to intercommunicate but there was huge pressure to make a new system do so. Meanwhile the old ones had to go on working. There were endless disruptions from staff expecting systems to work that never did and who were becoming less and less adept with the old paper systems. Critical materiel supplies often relied on a diminishing number of low-ranking depot staff having distant memories of where something might be physically located at the back of a distant warehouse. The project was a year behind at the half-way point, costs were spiralling, and Elizabeth had been brought in three months ago – the third appointment to the post in fifteen months – to sort it out and get it back on track. Her boss feared yet another grilling from parliamentary committees and spending watchdogs. He knew he was being closely watched.

Elizabeth arrived to find a demoralized staff, a remarkable number of consultants' reports, and a continuous – though not unusual – churn of key personnel on the client side within the government department, as well as a complete absence of strategic planning. The appointment had been a major career step for Elizabeth. Known to be searingly bright at seeing ways of understanding and simplifying complex IT systems and a great team member, this was her first job with full delivery responsibility.

She came to the first coaching session exuding a huge amount of energy, vivaciously dressed and apologizing that what was planned as a whole morning would have to be curtailed to an hour-and-a-half. She spoke almost faster than was comprehensible and started the conversation as if the coach was a member of the team and knew everyone on it by name and function. Elizabeth launched into an account of the initiatives she had under way and expressed surprise at the conversation with her boss that had brought her to coaching, though she had had a beneficial experience of coaching at an earlier stage in her career. Elizabeth said she thought it might be good to have a sounding board for a while in her present circumstances. So the coach sat back and listened. Under the torrent of information it was the wisest, safest and perhaps the only thing to do whilst trying to make some sense of what might be happening.

What he observed was a mind on the edge of chaos. What he saw affectively was a client running out of control; like a car on a hill when the hand-brake has not been pulled on strongly enough and it is beginning to gather momentum. He counted twenty initiatives that Elizabeth said were under way, all of which required her active input. He listened to the pattern of the seventeen site meetings she had set up, all of which she chaired. He discovered that she was travelling almost continuously around the country firefighting problems on an even wider range of sites, feeling proud of herself that she felt her brain was buzzing and she needed little sleep because she was so fired up. When the coach asked what her primary objectives were, who she had agreed them with, how she was getting her staff into shape to meet them, and what differences there were in what she was doing from what the previous incumbents of the post had done, she laughed and said: 'They were men and it's a woman whose going to get this one cleared up. I've got a free hand to do what I think is best. That was my single condition for doing the job.'

What the coach saw was a system in which different parts of Elizabeth's knowledge and skills were operating intensely at very different levels of skill and without any proper linkage between them, much like the individuals in the choir each singing their own song but not integrated – made cohesive or harmonious – by a single shared focus. Elizabeth's boss had picked up early warning signs of an emerging disaster, which centred on Elizabeth's firefighting activities. Her staff were becoming passively dependent on her active involvement in problems that only served to keep the old systems going. She had not identified any stakeholders; was therefore not communicating with them; and was developing an exaggerated sense of her own individual capacity to sort everything out. She had not worked out politically that her boss was himself having serious stakeholder problems and, in his own desperation, had agreed her terms for taking the job without either of them understanding the larger consequences. He had left Elizabeth with a free hand, generating an unrealistic level of trust in someone who in fact had no track record as a leader of dealing with the whole of such a complex and potentially highly volatile situation.

> What concerned the coach most immediately was Elizabeth's lack of sleep and her sense that she said she was buzzing so much that she did not need it. 'Look at Mrs. Thatcher when she was PM', she had said, with a slightly hard smile. 'She got by on five hours a night. I've got it down to four'. Everything about her affect was ringing alarm bells for the coach. She was not engaging him in any way at all. There was no resonating interaction. Everything seemed over the top: the clothes that were slightly too loud in colour for business dress; the flood of words and her incapacity to convey information in a way that might have meaning for the listener: the levels of activity: the hours she was working: the agreement she had with her boss to have a free hand and the way she was using it. Everything seemed wrong. It was not linked and not integrated. Bits of it were coherent but the whole was not in any way cohesive.

The coach had cause to be seriously concerned. He knew the brain cannot keep functioning on that amount of sleep, and that Elizabeth's behaviour and actions were a potentially toxic compound of Elizabeth using every bit of her considerable capabilities on demanding tasks that were mostly leading nowhere in terms of the overall task, and that certainly were not integrated into an overall picture. Instead of leading her staff she was substituting for them. The more she did the less responsibility fell on to them and the less she felt any confidence in them. She had not identified anyone who she trusted as a close colleague with whom to hammer out problems. She felt it was all up to her. No energy was flowing back to her. Her sleep pattern was evidence of high cortisol and **adrenaline** levels that, if they continued, would almost certainly result in a crash of some kind as she gathered more speed still. Elizabeth believed she was driving for a breakthrough, but the coach was seeing the beginnings of a breakdown.

He could reasonably and responsibly have insisted that Elizabeth's boss was right in wanting her to attend a medical appointment. Her boss was right that something was going wrong. But the coach also knew that if Elizabeth took a week off, and did go for medical care, it would be damaging to her own evaluation of herself – as she had in fact come for help in which she had some faith from a previous coaching experience. That had been part of a high-flyer programme. These were seriously different circumstances.

Taking the information/energy/relationships model of the mind that he was working with, the coach was wondering how he could create the conditions under which Elizabeth could get the brake back on in the first place; and then when things were under control and less chaotic how he could help her see what really had to be done. How, in other words, and for the time being, could he be the relationship that was missing?

With fifteen minutes to go the coach decided he would conduct a test. If Elizabeth failed it he would be insistent that she needed medical input and would not engage in coaching with her at this stage. If she passed it he would make what felt like a knife-edge professional judgement but one that, if the outcomes were as he hoped, would have hugely beneficial consequences for Elizabeth. So he said: 'Elizabeth, we have got only fifteen minutes left. Actually I need the whole three-and-a-half hours with you that we originally set aside. I don't know what the complications are for you to reset the rest of the morning, but we need that time together. If we can do that, then I think we might get somewhere together and I shall do my best to make sure we do. If we don't have that time, then I don't think there's anything I can do as a coach that would be of help to you except to let your boss know that in my judgement coaching is not the right course of action at this stage. Do we have the rest of the morning?'

Elizabeth went reflectively quiet for the first time in the session. Her coach had deliberately structured what he had said to give Elizabeth no negotiating room. He was being deliberately rigid to put tight boundaries around her chaos. He needed to know if she had enough capacity left to be coached at all. Using a metaphor he sometimes used to himself of the coach being like a mountain guide, he knew Elizabeth had got herself into a dangerously exposed position in which she had insufficient skill to manage the peril she was in; that he had not been involved with how she got there but it was his task to get her down by some means or another; that if she did exactly what he said there might be some hope for them both; but that if she would or could not he would not risk falling with her.

Elizabeth said: 'Well, it will be chaos, but if I can have five minutes I'll get my secretary to cancel the meeting I was going to. Why do we need the time?'

'Because of the chaos you're already in', said the coach.

'Well at least someone knows', said Elizabeth. The coach knew immediately that his judgement had been right. Elizabeth had enough awareness still functioning to respond as intuitively as she had in a way that told the coach she had some resonating capacity still left. They could work with that. 'Make your phone call', said the coach, 'and I'll get some coffee. Now we have changed the speed of the morning we shall see what we can do together with the next couple of hours.' A short break and some coffee was a way of changing the dynamics of the session. What he needed slightly more was a chance to straighten out his own thoughts about the next phase. Elizabeth had agreed to do what he wanted her to. He had to see how far he could get her to safety in that mood. And what, in practice, would safety look like? Then he smiled a little to himself and remembered that with Elizabeth's co-operation he did not have to do all the work. They could work it out together step by step. But first, the question of sleep.

'Elizabeth', said the coach when they had settled down again and were nursing mugs of coffee, 'how does it really feel, the way things are?'

'Really feel?' she said. 'I'm exhausted, it's a bloody impossible job, it will kill me or I'll get a decoration, but most of all it's so lonely. Will that do?'

'Not quite', said the coach, this not being the time for overt sympathy. 'If we're going to make it possible, get rid of the exhaustion, make sure it doesn't kill you, take a rain-check on the decoration, and work out what we need to do about the lonely bit, where would you like to start?' What the coach was doing was keeping Elizabeth in the state of co-operating with him as the guide at this point but also keeping her autonomy well to the fore so that the outcomes would be entirely her own. It would have been a great error at this point to be prescriptive – to tell Elizabeth what to do – for though she might have done whatever a coach said at this point it was unlikely she would have owned it. The coach's task, now that the brake had been applied, was to get movement in the direction of travel that was Elizabeth's, not his.

'Do you know', said Elizabeth, 'Alan (her boss) was righter than I let him know. A holiday is really what I need and I could get some sleep back. Even I know that four hours a night won't do me any good, though it seemed best to make a virtue of it as there wasn't any one to tell'. 'So where's the holiday to be?' said the coach. 'Today's Friday. How about you leave tomorrow or Sunday and come back next Sunday. You'll get a bit more than a week. Cheat the system, just this once.' And so she did.

How does the coach's brain create such a scenario, the details of which he could not know in advance but whose outlines were apparent from the moment he understood that the handbrake had slipped off? From the jumble of everything heard, as it is being heard, how is that shaped into the potential for another's experience? The answer is we do not yet know. It is part of the mystery of consciousness and creating resonance. But thought, reflection, courage, and the intention to be of service in the presence of the emotional presence of another person, allow a coach to use the accumulation of triumph and disaster from within the whole of a professional experience, and to craft the outline of a journey that has never existed before. For the brain of the person who comes for coaching has a unique landscape and the coach has the privilege of treading lightly upon it with that person. In coaching that is what affective integration is all about.

Summary

Emotions and feelings attached to experience create meaning. Without emotion there would be no meaning. So emotion underpins all decisions. The key source of influence between one person and another is managed by the way emotion – affect and the management of meaning – is transmitted and received between them. The emotional patterning laid down in childhood has been shown to have far-reaching consequences in adult life. The coach's task, in the adult life of a client, is to be able to pick up the energy of the client's emotions and use that energy to create a shift in the direction that the coaching contract has described. The means of getting there may be varied, but the principle of using the client's emotional energy to create the necessary shift always applies. The energy in the system gets reintegrated in the service of the coaching objectives. This is affective integration and it results in action and emotion achieving purposeful objectives.

9   Intelligent emotions

When Daniel Goleman published *Emotional Intelligence* in 1995 he established a public debate about the emotions that has fuelled a significant consulting and psychometric industry for nearly twenty years. His book appeared ten years after the term was first formally used by W. L. Payne in a doctoral thesis (1986), though there is a history of the concept being used as far back as 1966, and it is implied in some of Darwin's thinking about the emotions and 'social intelligence' in animals and man.

The development of effective **MRI** scanning in the mid 1970s, and its increasing availability for research purposes throughout the early 1980s, saw the beginning of what is now an explosive research interest in the neurosciences and the part that the emotional system plays in every aspect of our lives. Michael Gazzaniga's *The Bisected Brain* (1970) and *The Integrated Mind* co-authored with Joseph LeDoux (1978); LeDoux's own book *The Emotional Brain: the mysterious underpinnings of emotional life* (1996) that had been preceded by Antonio Damasio's *Descartes' Error: emotion, reason and the human brain* (1994) all began to make consciousness, emotions and the nature of decision-making hot topics. Other texts fuelling this interest included Allan Schore's monumental *Affect Regulation and the Origin of the Self* (1996) and V. S. Ramachandran and Sandra Blakeslee's *Phantoms in the Brain: probing the mysteries of the human mind* (1998). Taken as a whole this literature began to inform educated discussion about the emotional underpinnings of rational life in a way that nothing previously had done.

Consciousness and mind had been the province of philosophers, not scientists, but the 1990s saw that change radically in favour of the discoveries of the neurosciences. MRI scanning that produced black and white pictorial cross sections of the brain began to give way through the 1990s to fMRI scanning that showed coloured pictures and centres of brain cell activity. Popular as well as the scientific imagination was challenged by a new world of the brain beginning to open up. The Wachowski brothers' *Matrix* film trilogy, starting in 1999, picked up on the neurosciences allied to some quantum physics, as did the independent film *What the Bleep Do We Know?*, also of 1999, an existential enquiry initiated by William Arntz into the spiritual connection between quantum physics and consciousness. Somewhat earlier, and from a social psychological perspective, Paul Ekman had been working on understanding how emotions express themselves facially. His *Telling Lies: clues to deceit in the marketplace, politics and marriage* (1985) is one example of his extensive research and applied interest in the appearance of emotions. The clinically scientific and popularizing progenitor of them all was Oliver Sacks with *The Man Who Mistook His Wife for His Hat* (1985) that then became a one-act opera and subsequently a film too.

Now, around a quarter of a century on, the debate about what 'emotional intelligence' is has not been resolved. As with so much in psychology, it is characteristically one of those terms that lack scientific rigour even if they generate a great deal of debate and have some statistical underpinnings. At this stage the question 'What is emotional intelligence?' has resolved itself into three main streams of debate that describe:

- an ability model,
- a trait model,
- and one of mixed models.

They are worth exploring briefly to inform the shift that, for coaching purposes, we want to make towards the idea of *intelligent emotions*. Each of the streams have their commercial, as well as scientific, proponents though seem at times to be developing more in relation to consumer demand than the rigours of science.

EI as an ability

The ability model is the special province of Mayer, Salovey and Caruso (2008). Their definition of Emotional Intelligence (EI) is:

> *The ability to perceive emotion, integrate emotion to facilitate thought, understand emotions and to regulate emotion to promote personal growth.*

There are clearly difficulties here as the definition requires fine measurement to substantiate it and fine measurement is not a characteristic of the psychological sciences. In particular the possibility of accurately assessing personal growth has huge cultural, let alone metric, challenges.

The ability-model definition suggests that the main aims of emotions are to facilitate understanding: the implication being that this in turn facilitates the capacity to navigate social terrain – a concept not far removed from Darwin's understanding of the emotions. In an abilities model it is expected that individuals do vary in their abilities to handle emotional data and to integrate it into the whole perceptual framework that is particular to that individual. Four kinds of behaviours have been adduced as specifying the elements of the overall ability (over-arching categories of ability, as it were). These are:

- perceiving emotions,
- using emotions,
- understanding emotions
- managing emotions.

Perceiving supposes not only the capacity to perceive emotional states that are external to the perceiver – how your boss, your partner or the train guard is experiencing whatever is happening to them as you observe them – but also the emotional states within yourself. This is thought of as being the fundamental basic ability. Without that capacity nothing else can follow. The second category, using, involves linking emotional states to a variety of activities and adapting different mood states to different circumstances. The third, understanding, involves temporal processing for the understanding of changes in emotional states over time. And finally managing emotions is about harnessing emotions to reach intended goals.

The abilities model has generated a psychometric instrument called the Mayer-Salovey-Caruso Emotional Intelligence Test (MSCEIT) which is broadly available with a variety of options, including the opportunity to complete the test online, free or at some cost; the assertion that it is possible to find potential leaders by hiring people with high EI as assessed by the MSCEIT; and internet encouragement to train to use it. A quick internet search also uncovers critical comments from users (especially Steve Hein (2005) who has considered the matter of emotional intelligence extensively and critically). Whilst a good deal of work seems to have gone into refining the questions of the test, they lack the kind of objective scoring requirements of any standard IQ test and rely on consensus scoring criteria similar to a sentence completion test. In at least one formal study the MSCEIT results of 111 business leaders were correlated against their employees' descriptions of their leaders, who were rated by employees for empathy, ability to motivate and leader effectiveness. Ratings were shown to bear no predictable relationship to test scores (Føllesdal, 2008)

Within the same abilities framework are two psychometric devices for assessing emotional intelligence developed by Goleman himself some time after he first established the concept. They come within a competencies framework: the *Emotional Competency Inventory* (ECI) and the *Emotional and Social Competency Inventory* (ESCI) (see www.eiconsortium.org).

The ECI 2.0 site declares that it measures '18 competencies organized into four clusters: Self-Awareness, Self-Management, Social Awareness, and Relationship Management'. These clusters and subdivisions are as follows:

Cluster	Competency
Self-Awareness concerns knowing one's internal states, preferences, resources, and intuitions	**Emotional Awareness**: Recognizing one's emotions and their effects **Accurate Self-Assessment:** Knowing one's strengths and limits **Self-Confidence**: A strong sense of one's self-worth and capabilities
Self-Management refers to managing one's internal states, impulses, and resources	**Emotional Self-Control**: Keeping disruptive emotions and impulses in check **Transparency**: Maintaining integrity, acting congruently with one's values **Adaptability**: Flexibility in handling change **Achievement**: Striving to improve or meeting a standard of excellence **Initiative**: Readiness to act on opportunities **Optimism**: Persistence in pursuing goals despite obstacles and setbacks
Social Awareness refers to how people handle relationships and awareness of others' feelings, needs, and concerns	**Empathy:** Sensing others' feelings and perspectives, and taking an active interest in their concerns **Organizational Awareness:** Reading a group's emotional currents and power relationships **Service Orientation:** Anticipating, recognizing, and meeting customers' needs
Relationship Management concerns the skill or adeptness at inducing desirable responses in others	**Developing Others:** Sensing others' development needs and bolstering their abilities **Inspirational Leadership:** Inspiring and guiding individuals and groups **Change Catalyst:** Initiating or managing change **Influence:** Wielding effective tactics for persuasion **Conflict Management:** Negotiating and resolving disagreements **Teamwork & Collaboration:** Working with others toward shared goals. Creating group synergy in pursuing collective goals.

It will be clear even to a reader generally uninformed about the way social psychologists pursue their discipline, and perhaps slowly dawning also on anyone who has been deeply dyed in twentieth-century psychological thinking and practices, that much of this is tautologous. It has the appearance of being designed more to satisfy modern corporate fascinations with regard to leadership than contribute to a scientific and usable understanding of what emotional intelligence is. There is no basis for argument underneath observations that are defined by **correlative methods** that, by definition, define only association not causality.

So the question of whether, when you use the term 'emotional intelligence', you might be implying a set of abilities remains scientifically unresolved.

Yet the concept of 'emotional intelligence' does seem compelling. Before trying a different way of approaching it, the trait and mixed models merit description. The purpose in doing so is to make clear how muddled this widely-used concept is, how little practical value the working solutions connected to it seem to have and, most importantly, how little related to an understanding of the way the brain works they seem to be.

EI as a trait

'Trait EI' links a person's self-perception of their emotional intelligence with the idea of its being an aspect of personality rather than a set of abilities. A Soviet-born British psychologist, Dr K. V. Petrides, has published extensively in developing this approach (for example, 2001), which is backed by a widely-researched measure called the Trait Emotional Intelligence Questionnaire (TEIQue). It consists of the following fifteen subscales organized under four factors of:

- well-being,
- self-control,
- emotionality and
- sociability.

The Sampling Domain of Trait Emotional Intelligence in Adults

Facets	High scorers perceive themselves as . . .
Adaptability	. . . flexible and willing to adapt to new conditions.
Assertiveness	. . . forthright, frank, and willing to stand up for their rights.
Emotion perception (self and others)	. . . clear about their own and other people's feelings.
Emotion expression	. . . capable of communicating their feelings to others.
Emotion management (others)	. . . capable of influencing other people's feelings.
Emotion regulation	. . . capable of controlling their emotions.
Impulsiveness (low)	. . . reflective and less likely to give in to their urges.
Relationships	. . . capable of having fulfilling personal relationships.
Self-esteem	. . . successful and self-confident.
Self-motivation	. . . driven and unlikely to give up in the face of adversity.

(Continued overleaf)

Continued

Facets	High scorers perceive themselves as . . .
Social awareness	. . . accomplished networkers with excellent social skills.
Stress management	. . . capable of withstanding pressure and regulating stress.
Trait empathy	. . . capable of taking someone else's perspective.
Trait happiness	. . . cheerful and satisfied with their lives.
Trait optimism	. . . confident and likely to 'look on the bright side' of life.

Studies have shown that the scores deriving from the test are normally distributed and reliable. The traits are assessed by self-report – the person's perception of themselves – rather than through an attempt to quantify behaviours as in the abilities model. TEIQue scores have shown no correlation with non-verbal intelligence scores, as would be expected, but positive correlations with four of the 'Big Five' personality traits that are now generally accepted as the defining essence of personality measurement (extraversion, agreeableness, openness and conscientiousness); and a negative correlation, as again would be expected, with neuroticism and having a limited capacity to appreciate, understand and use feelings (alexythymia). Moreover in the quantitative genetic studies that have been carried out the trait model has revealed significant genetic effects and heritability's for all trait EI scores.

That is beginning to sound more like science and indeed the TEIQue is part of an ongoing research programme at University College London's Psychometric Laboratory. But still, does the fine distinction between abilities and traits (both of which are constructs of social psychology and personality theory not a set of neurological markers) help the pragmatic coach, who is not trained in the niceties of psychological theorizing and perspectives but is just after a way of thinking about emotional intelligence in the everyday life of a corporate client?

Mixed models of EI

Combining both traits and abilities, Bar-On (2007) has developed a measurement scale using the concept of 'emotional social intelligence' (ESI) – the ability to be successful in dealing with social and environmental demands and pressures. A total of 133 questionnaire items produce five composite scale scores that together yield a total Emotional Quotient (EQ) score. Bar-On considers variations in EQ to relate to social success if high and the likelihood of emotional difficulties if low. The scientific evidence for this has been variously questioned and the weight of evidence is strongly favouring the trait approach rather than the abilities or mixed approaches.

But these are only the main strands in a not-insubstantial field that seems to be as much consumer-led as science-derived. What should a busy coach do? What would be reasonably firm ground on which a coach might stand when so much seems tangled or scientifically muddy?

A starting point for coaches

A strong case can be made for saying that the existing models of emotional intelligence do not take as their starting point a sufficiently thought-through understanding of the way the whole brain works. Their starting points seem to be more the observational data of social psychology, personality theory and current management dogma.

One interesting way of using science as a starting point is Ian McGilchrist's *The Master and his Emissary: the divided brain and the making of the Western world* (2010). McGilchrist is especially fascinated by the balance of the differing functions of the two halves of the brain. The right hemisphere, he observes,

> . . . Has by far the preponderance of emotional understanding. It is the mediator of social behaviour. In the absence of the right hemisphere the left hemisphere is unconcerned about others and their feelings (p. 58). . . . It seems to me a possibility that those emotions which are related to bonding and empathy . . . are preferentially treated by the right hemisphere, as one would expect; such stimuli capture right-hemisphere attention . . . those to do with competition, rivalry and individual self-belief . . . would be preferentially treated by the left hemisphere (p. 63).

These observations become significant in the development of an understanding of the neurobiology of the Self.

> 'The personal "interior" sense of self with a history, and a personal and emotional memory – appears to be dependent to a large extent on the right hemisphere. . . . The right hemisphere seems more engaged by emotional, autobiographical memories . . . this part of the brain expands during the period of playful interaction between infant and mother in the second half of the first year, and the second year, of life, during which the sense of self emerges, and indeed the **right orbito-frontal cortex** is seen by Allan Schore as the crucible of the growing self. . . . It is also the right hemisphere that is responsible (Devinsky, 2000) for "maintaining a coherent, continuous and unified sense of self" . . . "emotion binds together virtually every type of information

the brain can encode . . . [it is] part of the glue that holds the whole system together (Watt 1998)."

(McGilchrist 2010: 87–88)

McGilchrist describes elegantly what are in effect the brain function foundations of Neurobehavioural Modelling, though NBM was in development before McGilchrist published. NBM relies upon an understanding that it is the limbic system, with the amygdala acting as the guardhouse to the brain, that is the distributor of emotions (and hence energy) throughout the brain, establishing the connectivity of event and emotion that combine to make for the consciousness of experienced meaning and the possibility of recall on demand. 'Emotion binds', says Watt (1998). In doing so the neurobiological self (though of course there could be no other kind) plays a, perhaps *the*, critical part in the organizing of the what, how, when and why the individuality of the self displays itself in the way that it does. For a coach, understanding this process is through due regard to the emotional process itself. This being so, the way into making sense of the internal world of the client, *for* the client, is to start from where the client (and the client's brain) *is*: not from where some statistical construct says it ought to be, divided into as many parts – eighteen, fifteen, five, four – as statistical refinements will have it.

That is in part why we have created the NBM process that relies on developing an understanding of the emotional biography of your client. From that enquiry you will discover a great deal about the way, and how well, the left and right sides of the brain harness themselves together – or don't – in the client as you begin to get to know them. Right brain is exploratory, left brain is certain. Right brain wonders, left brain fixes. Your right brain, properly exercised, will direct you into how to creatively link your brain to your client's. Your left brain's professional knowledge base as a coach lies in knowing that:

- there are eight basic emotions,
- they mix like the primary colours to create feelings,
- feelings are what give colour to life and meaning to experience, and
- there can be no change or development in behaviour without that change being structural in the brain and actual in the emotional pathways that create and consolidate that development, which are themselves manifestations of the Self.

That knowledge can be used in many different ways, but especially as an energy source from which to illuminate your own understanding of your client's brain and behaviour in your client's interest.

If emotions are a no-go area for the executive brain but an area of delight and discovery for the well-practised coach, how is it possible to bring a client's brain somewhere closer to where yours is? – especially when your client's brain has a long-established set of pathways that put emotions into a category connected with the 'not-good' rather than the 'good'. Start from where the client and the client's brain are most likely to be which (taking an informed guess based on a deal of experience) is likely to be in valuing intelligence, not emotion; yet with you knowing that science now tells us that the emotions underpin all decisions – a fact most recently evidenced by Nobel Laureate Daniel Kahneman in *Thinking, fast and slow*, his 2011 summary of a life's work on the non-rational basis of economic decision-making; and very usefully summarized by Jonathan Gifford in *Blindsided* (2012).

Do not create conflict. Start where the energy already exists – with thinking and information. But bring a little surprise into the process. Of the eight basic emotions, surprise is the potentiator and can produce a surge of energy that will start new pathways forming. Get your client wondering. Offer the idea to your client that the brain, considered by the Western world to act either rationally or irrationally, does indeed have two systems operating, but they both act rationally. That is to say, they both operate by a set of rules. It is just that the rule base of each is different and the rules of one allow it to operate much faster than the other. Would that be of interest to your client, to know those two sets of rules and the one that works fastest is the one less well known? It is highly likely that it would, even when it is established that the faster-acting part contains this funny stuff called emotions – and, incidentally, that the slower acting part does too, but with a different set of controls.

Such an introduction sets the groundwork for exploring with a client the possibility that what is key in a wide range of executive functions (and not least in those that involve interpersonal issues), is the exercise of intelligence underpinned by a working understanding of emotions. The approach we take to what is widely known as emotional intelligence is not, as is done throughout the corporate world, to present the impact of emotions as being some additive skill present in variable quantities and, by implication, at risk of being a lack; but as a summative attribute of the **cognitive processes**. Without the cognitive processes it would not be possible to appreciate the emotions at all. Animals can have emotions without any appreciation of them. In the corporate animal it is possible to increase the power of the cognitive processes by a proper understanding of the emotions that are key to the effective functioning of the cognitive processes.

An extension of what we mean here in terms of effect comes from the introduction to Sebastian Seung's 2012 *Connectome:*

> 'Genes alone cannot explain how your brain got to be the way it is', he writes. 'Your memories were acquired during your lifetime, not before. . . . Unlike your genome, which is fixed from the moment of conception, your connectome changes throughout life. . . . Neurons adjust, or 're-weight' their connections by strengthening or weakening them. Neurons reconnect by creating and eliminating synapses,

and they rewire by growing and retracting branches. . . . There is good evidence that all four Rs – reweighting, reconnection, rewiring and regeneration – are affected by your experience. We shape our own connectomes by the actions we take, even by the things we think. Brain wiring may make us who we are, but we play an important part in wiring up our brains'.

As a brain-based coach, part of the job is to know that the way you approach the brain of your client will either simply confirm it in what it already knows; or create the conditions under which its connectome changes itself, firstly because of your client's decision to be different and secondly because of your skill in knowing how to help the brain become different.

What we have described here with the idea of intelligent emotions is a way of taking something profoundly important in our understanding of the way the brain works – emotions – and re-defining the conceptual framework. In other words, moving away from what we believe is the essentially dead-end approach of defining emotional intelligence by a psychometry, backed by whatever academic discussion or commercial definition one might prefer, into a dynamic rather than a quantitative concept. 'Intelligent emotions' is, we find, a conceptualization that a client can move easily to incorporate and use in a wide variety of everyday situations; and that far from requiring a normative population honours, explores and uses the uniqueness of neural circuitry within any one individual.

David Rock's SCARF model posits the possibility that the human social brain is organized around its perception of Status, Certainty, Autonomy, Relatedness and Fairness. His 2008 formulation of the model draws upon social neuroscience to observe that 'much of our motivation driving social behaviour is governed by an overarching principle of minimizing threat and maximizing reward in groups, including all types of workplaces, educational environments, family settings and general social events'; and that 'several domains of social experience draw upon the same brain networks to maximize reward and minimize threat as the brain networks used for primary survival needs. In other words, social needs are treated in much the same way in the brain as the need for food and water'.

In the absence of any science of connectomics at the time, these are big claims, though the threat/reward hypothesis has been around psychology for almost as long as psychology has been around. The critical difference, however, between the need for food and water and social experience is that the first are appetitive matters and largely controlled by the old (reptilian) brain, whilst social experience is learned and is much more under the control of the mammalian and neocortical brains. Is it likely that they both operate under the same reward/threat regime? Snakes have appetitive needs that the snake brain meets very well; but snakes have no social needs – unless the tangled ball of a snake's occasional mating counts as such. Even if it does, the snake would not know.

A great deal of the experimental work in psychology to test ideas like the reward/threat hypothesis has been conducted on animals and especially rats which, though they permit high degrees of experimental control on a forced-compliance basis, are not known to give voice to their experiences. The much greater understanding that we now have of the emotional basis of behaviour makes it possible to revive an interest in the nature of experience as a means of enquiry. Experience that is (by definition) emotionally loaded can be understood through the framework of the eight emotions in a way that makes it possible to compare and contrast behaviours without recourse to generalized statements about threat and reward through focusing on the individual's perception of events. This also fits with the understanding that cell biology is formulating of the way the neurochemistry of perception provokes the genes into expressing themselves as they do within any one individual. 'Why doesn't he or she behave like me?' is answered not so much by reference to a reward/threat hypothesis but much more subtly by reference to the specifics of the individual's emotional patterning and its consequent perceptual framework.

What the SCARF model misses is a working understanding of the basic emotions, and especially that most fundamental of the attachment emotions, trust, which we left in discussing Elizabeth's predicament in Chapter 8.

Elizabeth

Experiencing pressure of the kind under which she found herself, Elizabeth defaulted to trusting only herself. This led to her demanding of herself objectively impossible outcomes whilst being certain subjectively that what she was doing was the only thing to do. There is no need to assume patterns of reward or threat to find a satisfactory understanding of what Elizabeth was experiencing. Occam's razor is a principle that applies well here – if there are competing hypotheses select the one that makes the fewest new assumptions until it is proved false. So understanding the processes that are linked to actions based on trust needs no assumptions of threat or reward at all. The coach's task was to create the conditions under which he deliberately tested Elizabeth's capacity to trust him, and then moved the energy connected to that into the action of going on holiday, immediately, that allowed her to realistically trust her own judgement and then to move that further into setting up the conditions under which she could begin to trust her team. In the background was the relationship with her boss, too, but the coach saw the unrealistic trust embedded there as something that would resolve itself if Elizabeth straightened out her own capacity to trust herself as a leader in the face of the stresses she was under. A brief holiday was like a tactical withdrawal in the military sphere. Regrouping one's forces is better than being annihilated, and Elizabeth did just that.

In other words the trust that came from the relationship with the coach then created the conditions under which effective decision-making could start to take place. This is where intelligent emotions come into play and how they grow. The emotions support the cognitive functioning as long as the emotions are properly regulated. Regulating emotions is like the capacity of a fine singer to sightread a new piece – seeing what the demand from the outside is and yet, at the same time, having a non-conscious and immediate sense of how each sung note is likely to create the next having itself flowed from those already past. A person who is emotionally regulating well does just that intraperson-ally and interpersonally every millisecond of their waking day, all day. They are tracking and factoring in emotions. When the day is finished and sleep has taken over then parts of the brain act rather like a sound recording technician doing some sorting out of the day's recordings. The live performance of the day has been given over to the splicing of the tapes into a coherent narrative from which wakefulness will start another day of living by means of, and yet further creating, the continuing story. Bad dreams, nightmares and early morning waking are as if the studio was not properly organized and cannot get its job done because of interference from one source or another. The emotions and the actions fail to integrate into the kind of memory traces that are the well-ordered product of a well-slept brain. Elizabeth and her coach created a chance to recover that state.

Summary

Throughout this chapter we have been writing about a coaching approach that stresses the experience of the individual within the framework of the emotions as the guide to understanding for both the coach, as guide, and the client as auton-omous voyager. Goleman's concept of 'emotional intelligence' has not been easy to ground into organizational use although, like many ideas of a similar kind before it, a not-insubstantial consulting industry has grown up around it. A good deal of this has been to find and purvey a metric that defines what 'emotional intelligence' *is*. There are now competing metrics with different structural under-pinnings. What may be useful in a coaching context is to work on the more pragmatic goal of developing intelligent emotions. Coaching experience suggests that clients find it easier to join up the idea of intelligence and emotion this way than trying to define 'how much or how little' emotional intelligence a person has.

10 NBM revisited

Throughout this book a number of clients have appeared in composite form. Coaching encounters with Jim, Simon, Andrew, Jennifer, Edward and Elizabeth have been described in order to ground the principles and practice of Neurobehavioural Modelling. This chapter sets out, at our current state of thinking and experience, a working understanding of NBM as a coherent articulation of the key principles that have emerged. They are wonderfully uncomplicated but, we think, equally profound in the sense that, if they are put into use, they will transform your understanding of your client, your client's understanding of themselves, and the way you coach. You will be continuously informed by your own developing understanding of how the brain works, how it will work for you in coaching, and how relationship is the key to unlocking whatever it is your client wants to unlock.

For many coaches the brain seems too complex for a coach to acquire any professionally useful knowledge of how it works. One of the discoveries of complexity theory is that on the other side of complexity lies a new simplicity. What we have wanted to do in developing Neurobehavioural Modelling is to see if we could get on to the far side of complexity. It is, we believe, the first practical applied neuroscientific model to try to do this in coaching. If it proves itself to be as good as a model-T Ford we shall be satisfied, or even as good as Karl Benz's first machine to which we referred in Chapter 5. That will mean not only that the design was essentially right but, more importantly, so was the conceptual framework underlying it. Put into use, NBM might splutter a bit, not be as sleek as one day it might be, and lacks a development department at this stage. But early road-testing suggests it is robust enough for daily use and shows a way of harnessing energy in a manner that has not been seen quite like this before.

Neurobehavioural Modelling describes the process where you, as a brain-aware coach, create the conditions for your client to model a change or development in behaviour – whether that is actual observable behaviour, or thinking, or feeling – that can then be tested, extended, developed and consolidated in the world outside the coaching session. Through the experience within the coaching session, reflected in changes within the function and structure of the brain, your client can consolidate that modelled change, through practice, in the course of everyday executive life.

Thus far then, the principles for the practice of NBM are as follows:

1. *Start from an understanding of the way the brain works rather than simply using bits of knowledge to justify what you already know. This means junking many twentieth-century assumptions often used in an unquestioned way as explanations of why people behave the way they do. The key to brain-based coaching within a neurobehavioural framework is to understand, catch, use and regulate your client's emotional energy, whatever it is, in pursuit of the coaching goals. There is nothing else to work with but energy mobilized by your client's experience of the coaching relationship.*

As an example consider the discussion of Elizabeth's coaching, and particularly the reward/threat assumptions that underpin so much thinking about human behaviour. We are not convinced it is an accurate, necessary or sufficient understanding of the way the brain organizes itself. Animal experimental models of behaviour miss out on the key component of perception that is so critical in the human condition. Or take another example. Often when someone is not doing what another wishes them to do, the idea of 'resistance' is brought into the conversation as an 'explanation' of what is going on in the recalcitrant person. It is the kind of idea that would be used if a client was discussing the problems in getting an unco-operative team member to change. Reconsidering this from the point of view of the way the brain works, we can observe that 'resistance' is not one of its attributes. It becomes apparent that using such a word implies your acceptance of an experiential, social and psychoanalytically-derived assumption that leaves you, the coach, with few options for action except to try to find ways to 'overcome' the 'resistance' whilst (secretly) (perhaps) agreeing with your client about the team member's intransigence. However, when you start asking yourself what your client or the team member *is actually doing* in terms of the experienced feelings and emotions he or she is having, then you enter the energy system that is creating their actions with some hope of creating change because you can redirect the flow.

2. *Action is always purposeful even if to an outside party it appears wrong-headed, misguided or self-destructive. A person never makes mistakes.*

It is inconceivable that the brain would operate in such a way that it made wrong choices. There could not be any evolutionary advantage in such a course of action. How then do we account for what we call mistakes? Why don't recidivist criminals, for instance, learn from their repeated 'mistakes'?

The brain has no templates for how things 'should be'. All a brain knows is what it knows. How it arrives at what it knows is entirely the result of its own completely unique experience modified by all its prior experience attached to its own genetic potential. With some brain cells (Purkinje cells) having the possibility of 100,000 dendritic connections, it is unlikely that science will unravel the specific neural pathways of complex behaviours in the near future, if ever. But even if science does achieve that remarkable feat it will not alter the basic position that the brain organizes itself the way it organizes itself out of experience, and it would not organize itself to make mistakes. It arranges itself to make the best judgement it can in any situation at any point in time. It may be to other observers – and perhaps even, a second later, the person themself – that the choice appears as a mistake in the light of a particular outcome. But that does not alter the proposition that at the time the person made the choice it could have been no other: otherwise it would have been. It is in this sense that the brain never makes a mistake because it is always operating from its own unique set of rules.

This is an extremely important principle. The retrospective classifying of something as a mistake can leave both client and coach in a complete cul-de-sac of which neither are properly aware through having colluded in a retrograde analysis of a situation from 'here' – i.e., with the knowledge of outcomes, rather than from 'there' – i.e., before the decision provoked the outcomes. Change in a client comes from being able to see 'there' in a way that the client, having been a committed participant in their own unquestioned action, could not have seen until a new angle of observation, grounded on the facts of the experience allied to the way the brain works, managed by the coach, makes a shift of perception possible.

3. *All behaviour is the result of, and is subject to modification by, the way we see things (perception).*

Genes control our behaviour, though they have absolute control only in the first three months of embryonic life. That is when they are directing the dividing cells to form the unique individual to which the newly-conjoined male and female chromosomes have given life. From the beginning of the fourth month onwards the genes that are contained in each of the developing brain cells of the body become increasingly subject to the external influence of the neurochemistry of perception. Initially, for the foetus, the mother's perception of her experience is biochemically created and is circulating in the blood supply of her intra-uterine life-support system and through the foetal brain. Then, when the infant is in the world in his or her own right, the growing child's continuity of experience creates emotional pathways that lead increasingly to expectations of how the world is likely to be as the myriad templates for that person are built up. It is how we see the world that creates the biochemical instructions for the genes to express themselves in the way that they do – subject, of course, to the presence or absence of genetic predispositions that have been laid down in the original mating. The major take-out from this for coaching is that *perception* is all. How we see the world is how our genes will be instructed to behave and how we become who we become. And that is why relationship is so important in coaching. The resonating of any limbic system with another is the means of opening up the perceptual world to the possibility of a change in perception and so a change in outcomes. It is the coach's skill to engage that mechanism into deliberate action.

4. **Biographical enquiry** *helps a coach to develop an understanding of a client's early emotional patterning and the way that has played out through life, which is the key to understanding any client. From this unique emotional patterning comes the way that energy will be uniquely directed.*

There are many occasions when the first coaching session is not the time to develop this enquiry. Some other urgency is apparent. But the first contact of any kind, whether by phone, email or in person, will be the start of a coach forming a hypothesis about what might have been happening developmentally to the client, getting their own thoughts running as to where those ideas might go. This process of enquiry makes explicit the fact that a client brings, in the brain walking in on two legs and settled in a chair, everything needed for the coaching session. The coach's skill is in working out what, of everything that is brought, is actually needed to achieve the outcomes for which the coaching contract has been made.

5. *Relationship is the key carrier signal between the coach and client for effecting any change or development. This is also one of the three fundamental propositions upon which NBM rests.*

It is in the coaching relationship that trust is established, which in turn opens up the limbic system to the possibility of creating new pathways, linking experience and emotion into new possibilities that in due course will be shown in the development of the individual as the consequence of coaching. Nancy Kline (1999) is perhaps the person whose work expresses this most clearly. Her discovery, in the thinking environment, of the way generative attention in uncontaminated silence allows the brain to explore itself such that it creates its own inner critique and options for change (or chooses to consolidate and reaffirm what it already knows) is a good example of the way a practised, deliberately-constructed and elegantly-managed professional relationship can have profound effects. In a coaching situation most coaches will not be skilled practitioners of her approach. But the operating style she teaches has a great deal to commend it as a way of simply learning how to listen to the other person's brain in action and stop the executive habit of apparent listening disguising a process of waiting for the opportunity to interrupt.

6. *Everything that happens has a neurochemical basis to it.*
Any client is a millisecond-to-millisecond dynamic neurochemical factory. The more you can observe behaviour and have in mind the main neurochemicals and their specific effects the more you will see them operating in your client and the more clues they will give you as to what is happening. For example, a dull look to the eyes suggests the stress of cortisol. The same, mixed with some agitation, suggests adrenaline being over-stimulated at the same time. Slumped body posture might make you wonder about sleep deprivation. A light in the eye at the end of a session suggests that something has moved favourably and triggered oxytocin. And so on. As you begin to build up your awareness of the minutiae of the way behaviours are the outward and observable effects of what the factory is producing so you may, if you choose, become increasingly sensitive to the inner world of your client that you are setting out to change.

7. *You do not have to know everything about the brain in order to start using what you do know.*
This is the principle of what might be called Occam's strop – a strop being the leather strap on which a razor is sharpened. Knowledge is sharpened by being put into use and tested and it is good to start by knowing how little you know and that you might be duller than you would wish. In use, that will lead to you demanding of yourself that you know more, until you find you know more than you ever thought you would. And then you will know how little you know. And so, most beneficially, it will go on. Like the best razor, your knowledge will always need sharpening and polishing, especially as the neurosciences go on to discover ever more fascinating and relevant things about the brain.

These are the seven principles upon which NBM operates.

It might be as well to think of them as the Seven Hobbits of Highly Effective Coaches – they are friendly, do not want to cause trouble, like being kept warm, live modestly and somewhat underground and in the background, occasionally need the help of a magician, but when the demand is made they will also go on the most arduous journeys in a good cause. They might make good companions for a coach.

And so it is time to see them in operation with Jim, Edward, Simon, Andrew, Jennifer and Elizabeth as we draw together our propositions and principles.

Jim
We left Jim raising by implication the question, for you the coach, about whether or not you would go on a difficult journey into unfamiliar territory with him. When a client brings the whole of themselves some of what they bring may not seem wholesome. Jim was showing signs of what the neurochemistry of stress can do allied to emotional patterns that allowed him to obliterate an

awareness of others, and so obliterate them by any means at his command when under stress. It is not surprising that, when under stress, individuals resort to their own safest, most familiar modes of operating – whatever the collateral damage may be to others. Stress has nothing adaptive about it in the sense of creating newness. Rather it draws on what is already well-established as the best bet for survival. So the fact that Jim could act as he did tells his coach that his actions were not a minor malefaction of the moment but were something that his system had in the past learnt to rely on and draw upon when needed in the present. Jim's actions also exemplify the second of the seven principles – in his own terms, Jim's actions were purposeful however destructive and self-destructive they might seem to others. The practical coaching question was, where to go?

A coach can only start with where Jim is. At any moment in time this might be viewed from a number of angles. It is the same Jim, but what coaching lenses focus the angle of observation? Jim's coach thought it might be worth testing out if his understanding about stress and its manifestations in Jim's behavioural system was near to the right target. It was, as he got the immediate sort of reaction from Jim that he expected. 'Oh God, don't talk to me about stress', said Jim. 'Of course I'm bloody stressed. It goes with the territory. Talk to me about stress and you'll have me off to some clinic in no time. No thank you. Anyway, Sally was a total bitch all weekend.'

Jim was behaving with his coach just as he behaved with Sally and at work. It might not have been quite so high on the obliterating scale but it was true to form. Having confirmed that he was on the right track the coach could find the way in.

'What shall we call it, then', he said, 'on the basis that's it's only you thinking about clinics, not me?'

'God I don't know', said Jim, staying in obliterating mode. 'You're the bloody expert. You tell me.'

'Well I could', said the coach, 'but you wouldn't be listening and we would only have a bit of a battle about whether you were right or I was even if you don't know what *it* is. In any event, it doesn't really matter what I think right now. It's how you see things that counts. Could you tell me?' And Jim did. 'It's bloody awful', he said. 'That will do', said the coach. 'We've got a name for it. Awful is as awful does. Tell me more about awful. Male or female would you say?'

The coach is freewheeling here, albeit with the NBM framework in mind. None of this could have been planned. Tactically Jim's coach wants to use the energy that Jim's emotions are creating to get where he, the coach, wants Jim to go – which is to shift Jim's perception of himself in his situation. Simplistic ideas like 'Jim should take responsibility for his part in the weekend or what he does to subordinates' would get the coach nowhere. They are ideas that come from a fantasy view of how human beings 'should' be. If Jim were to regulate his emotional systems properly, a *consequence* might be that he did take personal responsibility for his actions. That would be one among many other beneficial effects, of which the greatest might be a stronger sense of happiness, a marriage revived and a job saved. But those are not the focus of brain-based coaching through Neurobehavioural Modelling, any more than a surgeon setting a leg well because the boy who has the break wants to play rugby or kick his sister. With a well-set leg he can do either, neither or many other things. So it is with Neurobehavioural Modelling in coaching. The coach's task is to help the client reset the system or to develop it with one output being that of attaining the goals of coaching but in the knowledge that there will be many more effects than can be pre-determined.

Jim's coach had found a way in with 'awful'. By personalizing it he was surprising Jim. Making it male or female added to the surprise. Jim started joining in. The coach had begun to establish trust about the direction of the journey even if he had less sense of where he was actually going than Jim might have liked (had he known). The coach had been on lots of journeys before and so trusted himself and that is what made the free-wheeling possible – lots of energy but not a lot of control. It can be catching, and Jim caught it.

'Both', he said, 'now you mention it. You don't know what shape it's going to come in. Would hermaphrodite do, of the most horrible kind?'

Jim's coach was listening to the 'you's' that kept coming, as if Jim himself took no ownership for the particularity of his own experiences and might even assume that the coach already knew them. He wondered whether it was the right time to make Jim aware that they were jointly talking about Jim's experience not a common understanding; but he decided that they could come back to this later or in another session. There would be plenty of opportunity, the way he saw Jim's brain working. That decision was made because the other thing he noticed seemed, in the instant, more urgent. It was the posture that Jim had adopted. He sat, leaning forwards, hands on cheeks and fingers curled into his hair, looking at his shoe caps. 'It's not good is it?', said the coach. 'I told you it was bloody awful and now you know', said Jim, and began to cry. The coach had not expected to arrive with a Self so fluid so soon, but taking as much advantage of the situation as he dared said: 'And what would the name be for it when it wasn't Awful?'. Jim said: 'You've got me there. I've no idea.' And the coach said: 'Then we have something to find together. Why don't I get some coffee and we'll start'.

In the course of the conversation Jim's emotional state and its neurochemistry has changed. From high stress cortisol when he arrived, to a shot of oxytocin at the beginnings of trust based on surprise, to the adrenaline of bits of challenge to pressing forwards when the tears came, into something that was shared as more oxytocin and attachment flooded in. Jim and his coach have agreed to engage together. There is a relationship that has some joint energy in it and Jim has had the experience of his emotional system being regulated by the coach. He does not consciously know that in its detail, but he has experienced it. They have formed the beginnings of a relational bond that might have the power to make change. Principle 5 is especially at work.

Edward

Edward had discovered that giving his brain an invitation was much better than forcing its direction when he wanted its energy to try out something that was unfamiliar to him. What Edward's coach wanted to find out was whether that experience linked to his personal life would generate into the corporate situation too. What the coach had not paid enough attention to were the opposing forces in the firm.

Although it is true that the only person anyone can change is themself, in the early stages of change the circumstances or environment may well conspire to inhibit or kill the first flowerings of change. Like a badly-timed frost will wreck an apple orchard, so a client trying out new ways of dealing with his world may get badly frosted too. This is what happened to Edward. After his delight at experiencing how he dealt, during the coaching session, with the opera trip and his girlfriend's delight that evening, he went to the office the next day with a plan in mind to invite the difficult and acquisitive colleague to sit in on a new project deal with him, one that he badly wanted to join. For Edward it was a high-risk offer. He knew his colleague would be desperate to be there, wasn't certain what his added value would be, thought the firm would see it as a good move around the collaborative agenda, and was enthusiastic about trying out his plan. So he looked into his colleague's office and said: 'How about joining me on the project negotiation next week?' To his chagrin his colleague replied with a profound lack of grace: 'You're only saying that because you've been told to.'

We could speculate why that might have been the reply and in the development of his understanding of other people Edward might at some stage benefit from such speculation. But in context he was immediately wrong-footed and at a complete loss for words. He had been imagining the same kind of follow-through as he had experienced within himself – a loosening up in the relationship and a welcoming acceptance. He said, in some confusion, 'If that's what you think there's nothing to be said', left his colleague's office feeling humiliated and rang his coach.

The coach berated himself, internally, for having let Edward go too lightly into a lion's den. He had enough data from the biographical enquiry, and from knowing how Edward and his girlfriend inter-related, to have been able to predict that Edward would unrealistically expect his colleague to be co-operative. But his coach had got caught up in Edward's excitement and was not as thoughtful as he might have been. Principle 4 was breached. It would have been sensible, retrospectively, to have tried out some imaginal scenarios with Edward.

To stabilize the situation, the coach said: 'Fifteen all'. 'I'm not quite sure what you mean', said Edward. 'Well, said the coach, 'the idea you had about giving an invitation worked very well when you got your own brain to shift, but it didn't immediately shift your colleague's brain. Maybe it came as a surprise to him. Maybe he's feeing a bit more tender than you were aware of about finding you in the lead and in a position to make an offer to him. Maybe maybe maybe. We don't really know. What you and I have to work out is whether you want to stay with the invitation idea or not. And if you do, in what form.'

The notion that Edward was in the lead countermanded the humiliation he was feeling. The coach was pulling on the experience of delight that Edward had had in his own previous discovery and linking it to Edward's sense of being in the lead then. He hoped Edward would choose to stay with the invitation idea. And he did. 'Let's see how we can work it out', said Edward. 'What's to be done?' 'I don't know immediately', said the coach, 'let's see what we can do together.' And in saying that he settled Edward back into his own attachment feelings, which is always a position from which thinking can happen at its most creative. 'Well, what I could do is go and explain to Brian (his colleague) that actually that wasn't the way it was, that I was slightly thrown by his comment, and of course while there's a corporate agenda it was a genuine offer and I hadn't been told to do it. Would that do?' The coach thought that was fine, and Edward committed himself to doing just that. Which he did, and it worked. Brian was booked in for the negotiating meeting. Which gave his coach a chance to do some role-play work with Edward as to how he and Brian would prepare for that meeting; how they would work out their respective roles together; how they would inform the client as to their respective roles when they had sorted them out in preparation for the negotiating meeting; and how, whatever the outcome, they would debrief themselves. These were all new actions for Edward and well within the framework of his coaching contract.

Simon

Simon is not going to detain us. We left him having confirmed his own view of the way he preferred to manage his world, whilst noting that a little residual doubt might create enough irritation at a later stage to perhaps start a pearl growing. Or he might stay as a perfectly happy bivalve as he was. Principle 3. would work its way out one way or another.

Andrew

Andrew is typical of senior corporate clients where politics becomes part of their everyday existence. It is a corporate disorder that feeds upon itself. It is triggered by brains trying to make sense of other brains when the data is sparse, the trust is low, and the outcomes have high personal value. Any one of these conditions may exacerbate the political environment within a company. More than one increases the toxicity.

A great deal of time can be spent in coaching sessions analyzing 'the situation' and looking at it from all sorts of angles. When this happens with a client, give pause for reflection. Since perception is all and your client is telling you of his or her perception of the situation you might be tempted to offer alternate perceptions, as we touched upon with Edward's attempts to understand Brian. But such attempts will lead nowhere that is really productive in serving the coaching goals. They may create challenging conversations and a client may leave saying it has been a helpful session. You might even feel you have done a good coaching job and justified your existence. But you will not have changed your client or the situation to any significant extent because you will not have shifted the emotions. A client might well say, in response to your own interpretation of the situation, 'I can see exactly what you mean'. But it is what is unsaid that is crucial. Behind such a statement are unspoken parentheses: 'I can see exactly what you mean (but I'll stick to my own views thank you).' It is shifting the parentheses that defines a brain-based coaching job well done. It is the emotions that power the shift or maintain things exactly where they are.

In Andrew, what is observable is a reactive style. That always suggests that the Self operates in abstruse ways. It has been taught not to let itself become too apparent, to state its own needs only tangentially, not to identify its own desires too clearly. In consequence the Self goes about satisfying its own needs sneakily, often by apparently hiding or denying them – letting others make decisions and agreeing with them when they fit but not contributing much to the process; being critical and analytical but not contributory and inclusive; taking the role of observer rather than actor, a critic rather than an author or actor. Andrew seems to be like this.

In this instance, the coach's task is to help the Self become more Self-ish – or more self-regarding, if that is a more comfortable expression. There are times when the Self can only be looked after by itself and if it has not practised doing that then, when the need arises, it is left without the resources that it needs. Andrew found himself in such a situation, exemplifying Principle 1 especially.

Remembering that the coach's role is to act as regulator of the client's system until the client becomes self-regulating (in whatever aspect of the internal world is being developed), the task with Andrew is to start getting the self to articulate overtly, to make manifest its wishes and then learn how to act upon them. Sometimes that is best done in the way a knight moves on the chessboard, avoiding what is straight in front and moving sideways and forwards. So in pursuit of the undeclared aspects of Andrew's Self, the coach said: 'What is it you never seem to be able to find time for that you would really like to do?' Andrew thought for a little while, and then a smile spread across his face. 'Do you know, ever since I was a boy at school I've wanted to fly radio-controlled model aeroplanes. It seems a bit odd in a grown man, but Toby (his eldest son) is nine now. He might enjoy it'. The coach noted Andrew's immediate deflection of his own needs on to Toby, and said: 'How about doing it for your own pleasure and seeing if Toby wants to join in?' 'That's a strange thought', said Andrew. 'Why did, you say that?' 'Well', said the coach, 'if you do it for yourself and enjoy it, Toby has a chance of catching your enthusiasm. Then you are being the best kind of Dad, passing on to a child permission to enjoy the pursuit of a passionate interest through a relationship. But if you can only do it if Toby enjoys it then you will be getting your satisfactions through him when the wish to do it is yours. And if Toby doesn't get interested quickly enough it will jam your pleasure and Toby will somehow sense your disappointment and that leaves you both in a situation where you have no need to go at all. So why not do it for you and see what happens for Toby?' 'Done', said Andrew. And for the next half hour Andrew and his coach both played with their laptops in pursuit of all the information they could find about radio-controlled model planes that might get Andrew started. Coaching is hard work sometimes.

Jennifer
Jennifer was unlike both Simon and Andrew. She had no difficulty recognizing her needs, even though an earlier choice in life had led her to abandon some fascinations she then had for what seemed a more urgent need to earn well. And though that was not a decision she totally regretted, she had had some minor sadness at having cut herself off from what might have been a fine career as a scientist. Yet without difficulty she could balance the compensations that arose from the path she had chosen whilst maintaining an entirely proper sense of the 'what-might-have-beens'. Now she had been challenged professionally by seeing a way of integrating experience and previous satisfactions and needed nothing except a supervisor's minor direction to take her energies in a new direction. Which is what she did. She set herself big goals in the first flush of enthusiasm, finding the best master's programme in neuroscience that the University of London offered and then having to convince its head that taking someone from the commercial world was a sensible way of using a place for which there was high clinical demand. But she did. And she knew that in two years' time she would have re-aligned her way of practising to the extent that she could see some public expertise in a new field being within her grasp. Jennifer was enjoying her own neurochemistry, evidencing especially Principle 6. She could see a new harmony in her life – rather in the way that Prehn and Fredens Play Your Brain (2011) uses music as an extended metaphor for brain-based coaching.

Elizabeth
Elizabeth came back from ten days of holiday having slept almost continuously for the first four, and having been massaged out of her mind, as she said, for the

rest of the time. She returned ready to re-align her whole approach to the complicated project of which she had charge. Coaching was directed simply at that, using her energies in the best service of the strategic goals that she set about clarifying immediately. It supported her in the skills of learning to cope with ambiguity and uncertainty as she did so, whilst also mobilizing the energies of the staff she had inherited. She found out about their strengths whilst aligning those strengths with the operational demands she no longer felt she had to meet from within her own resources. At one coaching session she said: 'Do you know, I'm beginning to feel quite grown up.' The coach smiled, and said: 'Well, maybe at last you are meeting the person who has been waiting for you for quite some time'. Principle 2, had been especially in play between Elizabeth and her coach in the early understandings of what was happening to her.

Which leaves only Principle 7 without an exemplifying client. The fact is that all your clients have got to where they have got to knowing almost nothing of the brain and the way it works. And so have you. But you can be the bearer of new perceptions, able to open up to your clients the possibilities of the brain they were born with having more possibilities than they had ever understood. And that's because, if you become a brain-based coach, you will be operating the seventh principle for yourself first of all.

Summary

The seven principles of Neurobehavioural Modelling appear in all coaching relationships, but any one of them or more than one in any combination is likely to have special relevance for any particular client. A series of examples show how this plays out in practice.

Glossary

Action potential – a 'spike' of electricity which is the primary means of neurons communicating information to other neurons. Neurons that are generating action potentials are described as 'firing'

Adrenal gland – endocrine gland, above the kidney, releases the hormone adrenaline which has widespread effects throughout the body

Adrenaline – hormone released by the adrenal glands, involved in the fight or flight response of survival

Amygdala – almond-shaped brain structures in the limbic system on the inner surfaces of the temporal lobes. Act as a gateway, assigning and attaching emotional significance to all experience

Attachment – descriptive theory associated especially with the work of John Bowlby, attachment refers to the nature of the relationship between a child and primary caregiver, especially mother, and the life-long impact of various kinds of disruption to a secure relationship

Attachment emotions – primary attachment emotions are excitement/joy and love/trust

Avoidant attachment – refers to an attachment characterized by little or no contact seeking, response to parent seems unemotional

Axon – the long, thin nerve fibre along which an electrical charge flows from the nerve cell to release neurochemicals at the synaptic gap where dendrites of other cells may respond to the chemicals released. The main function of the axon is to send out information from the neuron. Axons can vary in length from being as long as the width of a human hair to two metres or more long

Axonal fibre – see Axon

Biographical enquiry – the process of learning about the individuality of each client through understanding the emotional bases of their life experience

Cerebral cortex – the outer folded layer of the human brain responsible for integrating sensory input and motor output. It consists of two hemispheres of folded grey and white matter with a bridge of fibres (the corpus callosum) joining the two halves

Chemical regulating agents – see neurotransmitters

Circuit – refers to neural connections which, through repeated use (fire together, wire together) become, in effect, a pathway

Codeine – an opiate derived from morphine and used for its analgesic and other properties. Less potent than morphine as a painkiller and a sedative and less toxic

Cognitive brain – concerned with information processing

Cognitive processes – the mental activities involved in acquiring, retaining, and using knowledge

Cognitive social neuroscience – or, social cognitive neuroscience (SCN) is an interdisciplinary field that asks questions about topics traditionally of interest to social psychologists (such as emotion regulation, attitude change, or stereotyping) using methods traditionally employed by cognitive neuroscientists (such as functional brain imaging and neuropsychological patient analysis)

Connectomics – the study of connectomes or neural connections in the brain

Connectonomics – see connectomics

Correlative methods – techniques which show a relationship between variables but do not indicate causality or give further explanation

Cortisol – hormone released from the 'adrenal gland' during stress. Known to alter information transmission in a variety of circuits involved in 'memory' and 'emotional' processes

Dendrites – one of the three main components of a neuron (brain cell). The dendrite grows out as a fibre from the cell body and is often highly branched, resembling a tree-like structure. It receives signals from the axon of an adjoining cell

Differentiation – specificity of neural activities

Diffusion tensor imaging – a new MRI approach that tracks water diffusion along nerve fibres, exposing the micro architecture of the brain, DTI can reveal major axon pathways and show physical connections between brain structures

Disorganized attachment – a display of disorganized or disoriented behaviours (by an infant in the presence of the parent), for instance, freezing or clinging whilst crying

Dopamine – neurotransmitter that plays a role in co-ordinating movement, in attention and in learning and in behaviours that are reinforcing. Serves as a main messenger in the reward systems, guiding behaviour towards food, drink, mates and all things useful for survival as well as acquired pleasures, including addictions

Dynorphins – a class of opioid peptides produced in many different parts of the brain (including the hypothalamus, the hippocampus and the spinal cord). They have many different physiological actions, depending upon the site of production

Emotions (basic) – those eight emotions (fear, anger, disgust, shame, sadness, surprise/startle, excitement/joy, trust/love) that are the primary source of energy within the motivational system and from which all feelings come. They are commonly held to be universal in humans though may have different social manifestations in different cultures. They also appear behaviourally to be common to all mammals

Emotional intelligence – originally conceptualized by Daniel Goleman as a wide array of competencies and skills that drive leadership performance with four main constructs: self-awareness; self-management; social awareness and relationship management. Underneath each of these lies a set of emotional competencies

Emotional system – it is suggested that emotion is related to a group of structures in the centre of the brain called the limbic system and other regions. Those areas currently thought to be involved include: the amygdala; prefrontal cortex; anterior cingulate cortex; ventral striatum; insula and cerebellum. Emotions are thought to be related to activity in brain areas that direct our attention, motivate our behaviour, and determine the significance of what is going on around us

Endocrine system – endocrine glands secrete hormone molecules into the bloodstream, where they circulate throughout the body. They produce testosterone, estrogen, growth hormones, adrenaline, thyroid hormone, and many others. Endocrine glands include the pituitary, thyroid, parathyroid and pineal glands, and the pancreas and gonads

Endorphins – produced by the pituitary gland and the hypothalamus, triggered by pain, danger and stress. They bind to their special receptors, altering pain sensations and 'mood'

Engagement – defined by the Chartered Institute of Personnel as 'a combination of commitment to the organisation and its values and a willingness to help out colleagues (organisational citizenship). It goes beyond job satisfaction and is not simply motivation. Engagement is something the employee has to offer: it cannot be "required" as part of the employment contract'

Enkephalins – involved in regulating nociception in the body, otherwise known as endorphins

Excite/excitation – Also referred to as 'activation' and 'firing', it is the process by which nerve cells use their 'presynaptic terminals' to stimulate the next receiving nerve cell in line to transmit information onward

Feelings – arise from the complex mixing of primary emotions that, by being attached to experience, give meaning to experience through conscious awareness

fMRI – functional Magnetic Resonance Imaging scanning techniques track the flow of oxygenated blood in the brain. Based on the premise that oxygenated blood preferentially flows to where it is in high demand, fMRI highlights brain areas that are most active when someone is thinking or doing something. Called 'functional' because scans measure how the brain performs tasks rather than simply mapping out the structure of the brain

Glandular system – the group of glands that secrete a particular substance(s), for instance a hormone

Glial cells – from the Greek for 'glue', glial cells comprise two-thirds of all brain cells. They serve various supporting functions to facilitate the optimal functioning of neurons

Hormones – a substance that is secreted into the blood at one location and transported to another, where it exerts an effect on the target organ. The various glands, situated throughout the body, are the principal sources of hormones

Hypothalamic-pituitary-adrenal (HPA) axis – a complex sequence of interactions between the hypothalamus and the pituitary and adrenal glands: part of a system that controls reactions to stress and the regulation of many of the body's processes

Inhibit – also known as 'suppression', it is the process by which some cells use their terminals to stop the receiving cells from relaying information. When a neuron receives enough inhibitory signals from other neurons, it becomes less likely to fire

Insecure attachment – encompasses two of the attachment categories: avoidant and resistant/ambivalent. Insecurely attached individuals have experienced inconsistent or emotionally distant care-giving

Interpersonal neurobiology – an interdisciplinary approach aiming to explain both our subjective and interpersonal lives. Draws on many different branches of science and posits that relationship experiences have profound influence on the brain

Left hemisphere – specialized for speech sounds, and understanding of meaning, it appears to be better at dealing with familiar information than the right hemisphere. Held to be more rational than the right hemisphere

Limbic system – a set of structures located deep inside the brain held to be the brain's emotional centre

Localisation – the process of assigning particular areas of the brain to specific functions and vice versa

Mammalian brain – otherwise known as the limbic brain

Mind – conceptualized by Siegel as emerging from the activity of the brain and in particular from patterns in the flow of energy and information within and between brains

MRI – magnetic resonance imaging is a technique that detects the magnetic resonance of molecules in the brain and uses this as the basis of images produced

Myelin – a fatty protective coating wrapped around long axons which facilitates signal transmission along the axon, greatly enhancing and improving transmission of information. (Myelin is white; hence the term 'white matter'

as opposed 'grey matter' which includes all the neurons and short local non-myelinated pathways)

Neocortex – from the Greek for new (neo) and the Latin for rind (cortex) the neocortex is the largest and most recent part of the human brain and is the outer layer of the cerebral hemispheres

Nerve cell – see neuron

Neurobehavioural modelling – using a working knowledge of the brain and mind to interact with another to create changes within the brain of the other so that (as appropriate) behaviour changes, the self is modified and these are both consolidated and sustainable

Neurochemicals – see neurochemistry

Neurochemistry – concerned with the electrically-stimulated chemical processes occurring within the central nervous system

Neurons – a type of electrically-excitable nerve cell located in the brain each consisting structurally of a cell body having many dendrites and a single branching axon. Information is transmitted in the form of action potentials

Neuroplasticity – the ability of neurons to forge new connections or make new paths; to 'rewire'

Neurotransmitters – the chemicals that are triggered by electrical activity in the brain cells

Noradrenaline – a neurotransmitter closely related to and having similar effects to adrenaline

Oxytocin – a hormone secreted in the hypothalamus, oxytocin induces a calm, warm mood that increases tender feelings and attachment and may lead us to lower our guard

Pituitary – gland forming the endocrine system. Secretes hormones into the blood stream

Plasticity – (see neuroplasticity)

Potentiator – the surprise/startle emotion from where it is possible to move to either an attachment or survival emotion

Prefrontal cortex – a multi-association area involved in planning, recent memory, abstracting, and categorizing information. It plays a central role in the forming of goals and objectives and then in devising plans of action. It is responsible for organizing things in time and involved in cause and effect considerations. Located in the anterior part of the cerebral cortex on the frontal lobes

Reptilian brain – in evolutionary terms the oldest part of the brain. It is responsible for sustaining life and is most in conscious awareness when it goes wrong

Resonance – Limbic resonance is the capacity for sharing deep emotional states arising from the limbic system of the brain

Re-uptake – after a neurotransmitter has performed its function (transmitting a neural impulse) it is reabsorbed by the pre-synaptic neuron. This aids the recycling of neurotransmitters, regulates the level of them in the synapse and controls how long any signal lasts

Right Hemisphere – research suggests that the right hemisphere's function is to deal with novel, unfamiliar information. It appears to be involved in the more subtle aspects of language such as nuances of metaphor or ambiguity and seeing the overall picture in any situation, responding to evocative situations with the appropriate emotion

Right orbitofrontal cortex – a region of frontal lobes of the brain thought to be involved in decision making and to have some involvement in the reward and emotion systems of the brain

Right ventro-lateral prefrontal cortex (RVLPFC)– located in the right frontal hemisphere. It is an area of the brain especially concerned with adaptive creativity

Secure attachment – contingent communication in which the signals of one person are directly responded to by the other. Requires that the caregiver have the capacity to perceive and respond to the child's mental state

Serotonin – neurotransmitter implicated in the regulation of 'mood states', including depression, anxiety, food intake, and impulsive violence. Also associated with tranquillity, calm, and emotional well-being, and consequently referred to as the 'happiness neurotransmitter'

Spindle cells – with a body about four times larger than other neurons and shaped like a spindle, with a large bulb at one end and a long, thick extension. It is thought that they are the secret of the speed of social intuition

Surprise/startle – primary (basic) emotion classified as a 'potentiator' since it might subsequently move into either the survival escape/avoidance or attachment emotions

Survival emotions – consist of fear, anger, disgust, shame and sadness (FADSS): so-called because, in association with glandular hormones, ensure fight, flight or freeze reactions essential to survival and so of great evolutionary and social significance

Synaptic gap – the minute gap between one neuron's axon and another neuron's dendrites. Neurochemical reactions are mediated across the synaptic gap

Synaptically – Synapses are essential to neuronal function: neurons are the cells that are specialized to pass signals to individual target cells, and synapses are the means by which they do so

Threat response – see survival emotions, a threat response is evoked by a perceived threat. It is a basic survival mechanism that includes the fight or flight response or freeze/paralysis response

Triune brain – a conceptualization of the brain as having three distinct sub-brains, each having evolved at a different stage. It comprises the reptilian, mammalian and neo-cortical brains

Ventral striatum – the striatum is a sub-cortical part of the forebrain and the ventral striatum is commonly held to have strong connections to the limbic system

White matter – see myelin, fibre bundles consisting mainly of myelinated axons

Wonder – to feel curiosity about, to desire to know, to express tentative enquiry: a manifestation of the surprise/startle basic emotion

Bibliography

Adler, A. (1924). *The practice and theory of individual psychology*. Oxford: Humanities Press.

The adrenal gland. Available at: http://en.wikipedia.org/wiki/Adrenal_gland (accessed 24/2/12).

Ainsworth, M. M., Blehar, E., Waters, E., and Wall, S. (1978). *Patterns of attachment: A psychological study of the strange situation*. Mahwah, New Jersey: Erlbaum & Associates.

Alert, G. (ed.) Power of a human brain. Available at://www.hypertextbook.com/facts/2001/JacquelineLing.shtml) (accessed 24/2/12).

Bar-On, R. (2007) www.reuvenbaron.org/bar-on-model

Beer, M., Eisenstat, R. A., and Spector, B. (1990). Why change programs don't produce change. *Harvard Business Review* Nov-Dec 1990, 158–166.

Berne, E. (1964). *Games people play: The psychology of human relationships*. London: Penguin Books.

Berne, E. (1972) *What do you say after you say Hello?* New York: Grove Press.

Bowlby, J. (1983). *Attachment and loss, volume I: Attachment*. New York: Basic Books.

Bowlby, J. (1986). *Attachment and loss, volume II: Separation*. New York: Basic Books.

Bowlby, J. (1986) *Attachment and loss, volume III: Loss*. New York: Basic Books.

Bretherton, I. (1992). The origins of attachment theory: John Bowlby and Mary Ainsworth. *Developmental Psychology* **28**, 759–775.

Canossa, M., Bergami, M., and Zuccaro, E. Molecular mechanisms of synaptic transmission. Available at://www.iit.it/en/neuroscience-and-brain-technologies/projects/molecular-neurobiology/molecular-mechanisms-of-synaptic-transmission.html) (accessed 23/2/12).

Casey, B. J., Somerville, L. H., Gotlib, I. H., Ayduk, O., Franklin, N. T., Askren, M. K., Jonides, J., Berman, M. G., Wilson, N. L., Teslovich, T., Glover, G., Zayas, V., Mischel, W. and Shoda, Y. (2011). From the Cover: Behavioral and neural correlates of delay of gratification 40 years later. *Proceedings of the National Academy of Sciences* **108** (36): 14998–15003.

Cherry, K. Structure of a neuron. Available at://http://psychology.about.com/od/biopsychology/ss/neuronanat.htm (accessed 23/2/12).

Coghlan, A. (2011). The 'rich club' that rules your brain. *New Scientist*, November 2011.

Cohen, J. (2012). Human brains wire up slowly but surely. Available at: http://news.sciencemag.org/sciencenow/2012/02/human-brains-wire-up-slowly-but-.html (accessed 24/2/12).

Damasio, A. (1994). *Descartes' Error: Emotion, reason and the human brain.* London & New York: Putnam Publishing.

Darwin, C. (1998). *The expressions of the emotions in man and animals.* Third edition, P. Ekman (ed.). New York: Oxford University Press.

Drake, D. (2009). Using attachment theory in coaching leaders: The search for a coherent narrative. *International Coaching Psychology Review* **4**(1): 49–58.

Egner, T. (2011). Right ventrolateral prefrontal cortex mediates individual differences in conflict-driven cognitive control. *Journal of Cognitive Neuroscience* **23**(12): 3903–3913.

Eisenberger, N. I. and Lieberman, M. D. (2004). Why rejection hurts: a common neural alarm system for physical and social pain. *Trends in Cognitive Sciences* **8**(7): 294–300.

Ekman, P. (1985). *Telling lies: Clues to deceit in the marketplace, politics and marriage.* W. W. Norton & Company.

Ekman, P., Friesen, W. V., and Ellsworth, P. (1972). *Emotion in the human face: Guidelines for research and an integration of findings.* New York: Pergamon Press.

Ellis, A., Eisenberger, N., Lieberman, M., and Williams, K. D. (2005). Does rejection hurt? An fMRI study of social exclusion. *Science* **302**: 209–292.

The Emotional Competency Inventory (ECI) and the Emotional and Social Competency Inventory (ESCI) available at://http://www.eiconsortium.org/measures/eci_360.html (accessed 24/2/12).

Emotional Intelligence; three streams of debate available at://http://en.wikipedia.org/wiki/Emotional_intelligence

Føllesdal, H. (2008). Emotional Intelligence as Ability: Assessing the Construct Validity Scores from the Mayer-Salovey-Caruso Emotina Intelligence Test (MSCEIT). PhD thesis and accompanying papers, University of Oslo.

Ford, M. E. (1992) *Motivating Humans: Goals, emotions and personal agency beliefs.* Newbury Park, CA: Sage.

Frankl, V. (2004). *Man's search for meaning: An introduction to Logotherapy.* London: Random House/Rider.

Freud, S. (1938). *Psychopathology of everyday life.* In A. Brill (ed.), *The basic writings of Sigmund Freud.* New York: Random House.

Gallwey, W. T. (1975). *The inner game of tennis.* London: Jonathon Cape Ltd.

Gallwey, W. T. (2002). *The inner game of work: Overcoming mental obstacles for maximum performance.* Great Britain: Orion Business.

Gazzaniga, M. (1970). *The bisected brain.* New York: Appleton-Century-Crofts.

Gifford, J. (2012). *Blindsided.* UK: Marshall Cavendish Business.

Goleman, D. (1996). *Emotional Intelligence: Why it can matter more than IQ.* London: Bloomsbury Publishing.

Harlow, H. F. (1958). The Nature of Love. *American Psychologist* **13**: 673–685.

Harris, T. A. (1967). *I'm OK, You're OK: A practical guide to transactional analysis*. New York: Harper & Row.

Hebb, D. O. (1949). *The organisation of behavior: A neuropsychological theory*. New York: Wiley.

Hein, S. (2005) *Critical review of emotional intelligence tests*. www.eqi.org/eitests.htm

The hypothalamus. Available at://www.wikipedia.org/wiki/Hypothalamus (accessed 24/2/12).

Jaques, E. (1997). Requisite organization: Total system for effective managerial organization and managerial leadership for the 21st century. London: Gower.

Kahneman, D. (2011). *Thinking, fast and slow*. United States: Farrar, Straus and Giroux.

Kline, N. (1999). *Time to think: Listening to ignite the human mind*. England: Ward Lock.

Kline, N. (2009). *More time to think: A way of being in the world*. England: King Fisher Publishing.

Koch, C. (2012). Neuroscience: The connected self. *Nature* **482**: 31–31.

LeDoux, J. (1996). *The emotional brain: The mysterious underpinnings of emotional life*. New York: Simon and Schuster.

LeDoux, J. and Gazzaniga, M. (1978). *The integrated mind*. New York: Plenum Press.

Lehrer, J. (2009). *How we decide*. USA: Mariner Books.

Lewis, T., Amini, F., and Lannon, R. (2000). *A general theory of love*. New York: Random House.

Maslow, A. H. (1943). A theory of human motivation. *Psychological Review* **50**(4): 370–396.

Maslow, A. H. (1954, 1987) *Motivation and personality*, 3rd edition. New York: Harper and Row.

May, Rollo (1969). *Love and will*. New York: W.W.Morton & Company Inc.

Mayer, J. D., Salovey, P., and Caruso, D. R. (2008). Emotional intelligence: New ability or eclectic traits? *American Psychologist* **63**, 503–517.

Mayer-Salovey-Caruso Emotional Intelligence Test (MSCEIT). Available at: http://www.unh.edu/emotional_intelligence/ (accessed 24/2/12).

McClure, S. M., Li, J., Tomlin, D., Cypert, K. S., Montague, L. M., and Montague, P. R. (2004). Neural correlates of behavioral preference for culturally familiar drinks. *Neuron* **44**: 379–387.

McGilchrist, I. (2010) *The master and his emmissary: The divided brain and the making of the western world*. New Haven, CT: Yale University Press.

Mischel, W., Ebbesen, E. B., and Raskoff Zeiss, A. (1972). Cognitive and attentional mechanisms in delay of gratification. *Journal of Personality and Social Psychology* **21**(2): 204–218.

Newton, R. (2008). *The attachment connection*. Oakland, CA: New Harbinger Publications Inc.

Payne, W. L. (1983/1986). A study of emotion: developing emotional intelligence; self integration; relating to fear, pain and desire. *Dissertation Abstracts International* **47**: 203A (University microfilms No. AAC 8605928).

Petrides, K. V. and Furnham, A. (2001). Trait emotional intelligence: Psychometric investigation with reference to established trait taxonomies. *European Journal of Personality* **15**: 425–448.

The pituitary gland. Available at://http://en.wikipedia.org/wiki/Pituitary_ gland (accessed 24/2/12).

Ramachandran, V.S. and Blakeslee, S. (1998). *Phantoms in the brain: Probing the mysteries of the human mind.* USA: Fourth Estate.

Rock, D. (2008). SCARF: a brain based model for collaborating with and influencing others. *NeuroLeadership Journal* **I**: 1–11.

Rock, D. (2009). Managing with the brain in mind: *Strategy + business* **56**, Autumn 2009, Reprint no. 09206, 4–5.

Rock, D. and Ringleb, A. The NeuroLeadership Institute. Available at: //http://www.neuroleadership.org/ (accessed 24/2/12).

Sacks, O. (1985). *The Man Who Mistook His Wife for a Hat, and Other Clinical Tales.* United States: Summit Books.

Schore, A. (1996). *Affect regulation and the origin of the self.* USA: W. W. Norton & Company.

Seung, S. (2012). *Connectome: How the brain's wiring makes who we are.* USA: Houghton Mifflin Harcourt.

Siegel, D. (1999). *The developing mind: How relationships and the brain interact to shape who we are.* New York: The Guildford Press.

Siegel, D. (2010) *Mindsight: The new science of personal transformation.* New York: Bantam Books.

Siegel, D. J. *The Neurobiology of 'We'.* DVD series, Sounds True: Boulder, Colorado. (www.soundstrue.com).

Skinner, B. F. (1938). *The behavior of organisms: An experimental analysis.* Oxford, England: Appleton-Century.

Sporns, O., Tononi, G., and Kötter, R. (2005). The human connectome: A structural description of the human brain. *PLoS Computational Biology* **1**, e42.

Trait Emotional Intelligence Questionnaire (TEIQue) available at: http://www.psychometriclab.com/ (accessed 24/2/12).

Watt, D. E. (1998). Affect and the limbic system: some hard problems. *Journal of Neuropsychiatry and Clinical Neurosciences* **10**: 113–116.

Index

The index entries appear in word-by-word alphabetical order.